*Dedicated to my father-in-law, Jimmy Griggs,
a wonderful example of a changed life.*

The

Third Chair

Implementing Lasting Change

JOE PHILLIPS

ISBN: 0615856713
ISBN-13: 9780615856711

ACKNOWLEDGEMENTS

Thanks to my patient and Jesus loving wife, Cecilia.

Special thanks to my son, Joseph, for coordinating this project.

Big gratitude to my other great kids, Lauren, Kennon, and Madeline.

Thanks to my administrative assistant, Jennifer Boyd, for proofing the book multiple times.

Thanks also to Kimberly Short for her input.

I am very thankful to Haley Doolittle for illustrating this book.

Thanks to Jewell Massey and her team of intercessors for covering this work in prayer.

Thanks to Concord First Assembly and Dr. Rick Ross, Lead Pastor.

Thanks to Pastor Doug Witherup for his encouragement and friendship.

Thanks to my lifelong friends Lee McBride and Jay Stewart and the journey of change that has been fun to watch.

TABLE OF CONTENTS

INTRODUCTION

I Have To Change

And he said: "Truly I tell you, unless you change and become like little children, you will never enter the kingdom of heaven."
(*Gospel of Matthew 18:3*)

DERECHO

Sometimes stuff happens, and plans don't work out. Like my plan of getting hotel rooms in Charleston, West Virginia, on my way from Charlotte, North Carolina, to Michigan, where I was speaking at a camp for the entire family. "Come on kids; this will be an adventure," I told three teenagers and a twenty-one-year old. I like rolling that way sometimes to shake myself out of my OCD behavior. When I am off to do a comedy show or a ministry event, I sometimes "wing it" with the travel. I will drive until it feels like stopping time. Well, I should have been a little more diligent in my planning this particular Friday, June 29. A "land hurricane" called a derecho had hit the United States from the Midwest to the east coast. It threw three million people into darkness. When people are in the dark and hot in the summer, where do they go? Hotels. Where did I go? Not to a hotel in Charleston, West Virginia, as I had planned, or even Marietta, Ohio, in the extreme southern tip of that state. I went to the only hotel I could find. In *Kent,* which is near Cleveland! That constituted about two or more extra hours of driving on this road trip. So as my two teenagers, one of their friends, and my twenty-one-year old daughter slept or worked on their devices during that all night drive, the Lord did to me what he does. He gave me a stream of insight for a sermon. That sermon has turned into this book.

I struggled that night with the insight for a few reasons. First, after driving in the middle of the night I wasn't entirely sure I was lucid! Also, I like to preach from one text—camp out in one Biblical text and dig out all the truth I can find. Plus, I am not big into "formulas," and as you will find out, this particular insight from the Lord came to me as something of a formula. (I joke around in my comedy events, "Please buy my *Get Rich Program.* Discover and MasterCard are accepted. It has two pages: Make more money, page one. Spend less money, page two. Get 'em while supplies last. Coming soon: *Weight Loss Program.* Two pages: Eat less food. Move your body more. Only one hundred ninety-nine dollars. Line up one at a time, please.") I don't trust formulas a whole lot, with a few notable exceptions (perhaps *7 Habits, Good To Great,* and definitely *The Holy Bible* formulas).

FAHOLO
I worked through the material in this book when we reached our destination in Michigan, a great campground called FAHOLO, named for the first two letters in each of the words *faith, hope,* and *love.* I was scheduled to preach that week, but I didn't really want to preach the sermon that had come to me on the drive up. I didn't feel prepared.

On Tuesday, July 3, I played in a three-on-three basketball tournament with my seventeen-year-old son Kennon. Then I played nine holes of disc golf. (Insert joke: "I have always said I would play basketball until I was too old and had to play golf. But no one told me that when I was too old to play basketball I would be too broke to play golf, and I'd have to throw discs.") I did all of that activity on forty-eight-year-old knees. So, in the lodge, reclining on a bed with two Ziplocs of ice resting on my knees, I finished handwriting this sermon. It was an aggravating act of sheer obedience.

Of the five sermons I preached that week this was the only one I did not have memorized. I typically only like to preach what I have committed to memory for some OCD reason. I carried my sermon book in my left hand while speaking. I walked around the chairs I had thrown in place at the last minute. Ten chairs to represent the ten chairs of change we all must sit in on the path toward transformation.

It was a powerful camp. Profound miracles happened. Two were financial. One man who had not spoken in ten years because of a stroke spoke sentences just days later. A thirteen-year-old boy who wore a harness because of a horrible under bite said, "Jesus pushed my jaw back." He wept as his father/pastor confirmed the miracle. (Later the University of Michigan's surgeons confirmed it as well, according to his father.) In all of these years of full time traveling, there have been many amazing happenings. There has been a good deal of encouragement also. Perhaps the most positive feedback I have received in all of these years came from this message you now hold in your hands. Dan, a dad and minister, said, "It changed my life."

So my next somewhat aggravating act of obedience was to produce the message in book form. I hope this simple, simple message will help you transform areas of your life that need to be transformed. This is a book about change and transformation. Each one of us needs to walk through the only guaranteed thing in life—change—with an intentional process. The change may be major, like quitting a life of addiction. Perhaps you think it's minor, like reading more instead of wasting time. It all matters. And the goal of this book is to help you put some framework, a process, around the change you need to make and to put some hope in your heart that it *is* possible.

I make just a note here about names. In the book it is possible names were changed where it seemed helpful to protect identities.

1

GOT CHANGE?
BEFORE CHAIRS

Do not conform to the pattern of this world, but be transformed by the renewing of your mind. Then you will be able to test and approve what God's will is—his good, pleasing and perfect will.
(Romans 12:2)

POPS

A few years ago, I had the great privilege of introducing my hero, my father-in-law (who is more like my own father) Jimmy Griggs, as he was inducted into the inaugural Jordan Vocational High School Athletic Hall of Fame. He had already been inducted into other halls in the southwest Georgia area. During the ceremony, in front of five hundred people, with the city leaders and media in attendance, inductees included a Kansas City Chief player in Super Bowl I, as well as an Oakland A's pitcher and the entire 1974 state champion baseball team.

But my biggest thrill of the night was when an attractive blonde lady went to the podium to introduce her own father and turned to my father-in-law. "Before I introduce Daddy I want to say this. I didn't know Mr. Jimmy Griggs would be here. Mr. Jimmy, I want to thank you publicly. You are responsible for my personal salvation. Thank you so much."

He was already in *my* Hall of Fame, but that night his picture got another spotlight. Jimmy's pastor, Paul Thomas, told me that those kinds of stories are all over Columbus, Georgia. Stories of people Jimmy Griggs has won to Christ.

NO BALL!

Jimmy grew up with a single mamma in the 1940s at East Highland Assembly of God in Columbus, Georgia. With all that was right in the church of America during that season, at least one thing was not. It was a sin to play sports. Little Jimmy, who would later be an inductee into various athletic halls of fame, loved to play ball. So he started sneaking around as a little boy to play until he could sneak no longer. Then he walked away from the Lord. He walked into the world, way into the world. He would serve at the end of World War II in Japan and come home to begin a life of alcoholism.

In 1969, when Jimmy was in his forties, he received terrible news. His beloved wife, Anne, was stricken with a brain tumor. Dr. Hazouri told Jimmy to be prepared to raise his and Anne's two little girls alone. That news pushed him into a hospital chapel, and when he came out of that chapel an old Sunday school teacher of his was walking down the hallway of the Medical Center Hospital. When she asked him why he was there, he shared his plight. The teacher told her pastor Jimmy's story, and consequently, two ministers walked into Jimmy's life. They shared good news. Anne survived and has lived a long life. The whole family came to know Jesus Christ in a very personal way.

Jimmy became an incredible intercessor - one who prays fervently for another - and a legendary soul winner. He was transformed. His life dramatically changed.

TRANSFORMATION

Here are some definitions of *transform*:

1) to change in form, appearance, or structure; metamorphose;
2) to change in condition, nature, or character; convert;
3) to change into another substance, transmute.

I believe in transformation. Change is the only certainty in life. There are good changes and bad ones, but change is guaranteed. My great and good father-in-law, Jimmy Griggs, was transformed.

MY HAND UP

I need to change. Well, I need to make a few changes. Spiritually, I need to grow deeper. Professionally, I need to reach more people in ministry with greater effectiveness. Physically, there are some things beyond my control. Fortunately, or unfortunately, there are at least a couple changes within my grasp I had better make. This book presents you with a formula for change. It might well be placed in the genre of self-help, but from the outset, let the record reflect, there are some changes that require a village. And the tribal chief of the village. And maybe a neighboring village auxiliary group. And the creator of all the villages. There are changes that can only be accomplished with the help of an outside entity—divine or human. Or both. However, that fact does not negate my responsibility in my own change process.

BREATH = HOPE

"Did you get a card?" I asked a friend in jail.

"No, Pastor Joe, what are you talking about?" he replied.

"You know, a card to punch?"

"What card?"

"Like at Subway, Ernie. When you get ten punches they give you a free sandwich. You've been in jail so many times surely you can get a few punches and get an extra pudding at chow."

He said, "No, I didn't get a card."

That was probably mean of me, and he didn't think it was too funny as he looked at me through the jail plexiglass. I wasn't trying to do stand-up. I wanted his attention. What I said next was not mean, and it is the heart of this book. "Ernie, stop coming here. I am sick of looking at you through plexiglass. But I want you to look through this dirty piece of plastic and into my eyes. I believe in God, and I believe in you. And as long as there is breath, there is hope. You got breath, boy. I got hope. Your situation can change!"

I do believe in the possibility of great change for human beings.

SAUL

Wise, old Samuel, the last Hebrew judge and first prophet, instructed young Saul, who would someday be king:

> *The Spirit of the Lord will come powerfully*
> *upon you, and you will prophesy with them;*
> *and you will be <u>changed into a different person.</u>*
> (*1 Samuel 10:6, emphasis always mine*)

Wow. In the English Standard Version, this scripture says the Spirit will "rush" upon you. He rushed upon me in 1982 and began a powerful change process, a transformation. Jimmy Griggs was transformed into a different person. From the drinker with a bottle hidden under his car seat to the winner of lost souls. Not every transformation is that radical, but even small ones make a difference. The Spirit can rush upon us for any change.

GOD ENDORSES

Think about this scripture for a moment. You read it under the chapter title but I want you to read it again slowly:

> *Therefore, I urge you, brothers and sisters, in*
> *view of God's mercy, to offer your bodies as a*
> *living sacrifice, holy and pleasing to God—*
> *this is your true and proper worship. Do not*
> *conform to the pattern of this world, BUT BE*
> *TRANSFORMED by the renewing of your*
> *mind. Then you will be able to test and approve*
> *what God's will is—his good, pleasing and per-*
> *fect will. (Romans 12:1, 2)*

Not only does God endorse transformation but he *expects* us to 1) change in form, appearance, or structure; metamorphose, 2) change in condition, nature, or character; convert. It sounds a little like a command. At the very least, it is a strong "urge" from the Spirit.

PLAIN OLE JOE

I'm a pretty simple fellow. I am happiest when things are easy to understand. Simplicity is brilliance to me. Like the latest communication technology. Advanced calculus may be required to create the devices, but even guys like me can use them. On that all-night Ohio drive, I stumbled into the simplicity of change, and I will do my best in these pages to make it simple to you.

Once I learn a system, I am likely to use it. Are you that way? We learn how to tie our shoes early, and we really don't need a continuing education curriculum to stay sharp on the process. *Shoes are tied this way. Got it.* I have learned a few things over the years and have signed the process adoption papers. They are established practices, just like tying my shoes, with occasional tweaks.

My hope is this book presents to you a process for change you can adopt, establish, and tweak as needed. *Change is accomplished this way. Got it.* Use what you can from these pages – these chairs of transformation - and toss the rest. Hopefully something will transform in your life that will help you and encourage others.

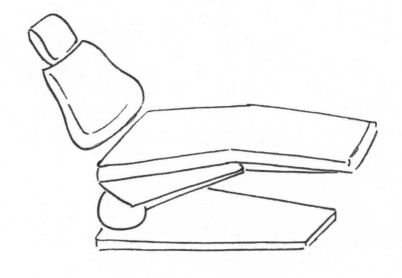

2

DIAGNOSIS
CHAIR ONE

He longed to fill his stomach with the pods that the pigs were eating, but no one gave him anything.
(Gospel of Luke 15:16)

CURE

In my twenty-six years of ministry I have been with countless families as they've received unhappy news. News that is sometimes followed by unhappy questions:

"How bad is it?"

"Is there anything that can be done?"

"How much time do I have?"

X-rays and lab reports bring to the experts a diagnosis. And this is the first step in receiving any possible cure. A doctor cannot get to the cure without an adequate assessment.

Diagnosis is the first, and really the easiest, chair for us to sit in. Most of us know what needs to change in our lives. The mirror shows us. The bank balance shows us. We see it in the climates and atmospheres of our homes. I tell crowds, "If any of you gets stumped about what changes you need to make, just lean over and ask your spouse. He or she will be happy to give you a hand coming up with an idea...or twelve."

DENIAL
Sometimes people put their heads in the sand like ostriches.

"I'll ignore this chronic pain in my shoulder, and it will surely go away."

"If I don't face the lab report, maybe it is not real."

"If I don't answer the door, maybe those uniformed men will go away, and that means my loved one has not passed away."

Pain is pain. Sadly the lab is the lab. Bad news stays on the porch until it is dealt with. Our diagnoses must be addressed.

I had a friend once, an outstanding young man and a great minister, especially to youth. My wife noticed one day that he was favoring one of his arms and drawing up the other one. She encouraged him to get it checked out. He went a long time without seeing a doctor. He didn't have insurance. He hoped it would go away. Finally he did seek medical advice and found out he had a rare disease causing this and other symptoms. It was a horrible day when I had to speak at his funeral. He was an incredible talent and only in his twenties when he died. An early diagnosis may or may not have helped him. For most needed changes, however, diagnosis is foundational, and the earlier the diagnosis, the better.

POD X-RAY

A kid, known by the unhappy moniker of "the Prodigal Son" wanted his money. He demanded it. He got it. He wasted it. Then a diagnosis presented itself:

> *After he had spent everything, there was a severe famine in that whole country, and he began to be in need. So he went and hired himself out to a citizen of that country, who sent him to his fields to feed pigs.* <u>*He longed to fill his stomach with the pods that the pigs were eating,*</u> *but no one gave him anything.* (Luke 15:14-16)

Diagnosis? Hunger! If you've never really, really been hungry it will be difficult to understand this focused diagnosis. This boy was sho' nuff (as we say down south) hungry. Secondary diagnosis? Indentured servitude. When the man began to dream about the disgusting food the pigs ate, well, he knew he was in trouble. And something gloriously mean happened that would prove pretty important in his change: "No one gave him anything." Haven't you learned that, although help is available, enabled people change at a glacier pace and often do not change at all? Real change movement happens at the corner of Bad Days Boulevard and Stand Alone Avenue.

RARE CHAIR

Diagnosis is the very starting point of all great change. Unfortunately for too many, it is the alpha *and* omega, the first *and* the last. People often never get beyond the knowing or awareness. "I need to lose weight. Where are those Cheetos?" Sitting in the first chair won't magically move you down the line toward the tenth chair. The chairs of transformation have no rollers on them. Chair one simply crystalizes the need for change.

On occasion we don't know what we need. Life is complicated, and we cannot always put a finger on the exact problems. In those rare moments, divine intervention is needed. I remember being on the side of a mountain at a men's retreat. We were in a "monastic fast": two bottles of water and two bottles of Gatorade with strict instructions to not utter a word from the moment we awoke until eight pm. On November 5, 2009, during that fast, the Holy Spirit revealed to me a diagnosis to which I had been oblivious. I was wrong—dead wrong—in an area of my life affecting my ministry and my family. I had unrealized emotions concerning my relationship with my dad. I repented and moved down the line to change. That kind of experience is rather rare. Most changes I need to make are in the front of my mind – not the back. I need not send out a search party. I trip over the needed changes.

DR. YOU

What would you like to change right now? If you could wave a wand and change one thing, what would it be? What about three things? Imagine what change would look like. At the risk of sounding like a self-help guru or a direct marketing expert, these are the questions I need to ask you. Jesus asked them:

> *"What do you want me to do for you?" he asked.*
> *(Matthew 20:32)*

> *"What do you want me to do for you?" he asked.*
> *(Mark 10:36)*

> *"What do you want me to do for you?" Jesus asked*
> *him. The blind man said, "Rabbi, I want to see."*
> *(Mark 10:51)*

> *"What do you want me to do for you?" "Lord, I*
> *want to see," he replied. (Luke 18:41)*

A man wanted to see. He had already diagnosed himself. So when opportunity presented itself, it wasn't difficult for him to tell the Lord what change needed to be made. Do you know what you would say if Jesus asked you that question?

"What do you want me to do for you?"

"I'm good, thanks, Lord."

"Sure about that?"

"Yep."

Well, if Jesus ever asks *me* this question, I have a 'Need to Change' list memorized! Successful people always work on themselves and push the needle toward good transformation.

YOU RUN YOU

I am responsible for neither the conformation nor dysfunction in other people. And it is all around me. However, I am responsible for my own function and for my own transformation. I can't change your dysfunction when I have so much work to do on my own dysfunction. But with God's help, transformation is possible for both of us.

I'M THE DUMBEST

A man named Gideon had an easy diagnosis. People were about to die. The Lord approached him, and his dismal diagnosis went like this:

> **The angel of the Lord came and sat down under the oak in Ophrah that belonged to Joash the Abiezrite, where his son Gideon was threshing wheat in a winepress to keep it from the Midianites..."Pardon me, my lord," Gideon replied, "but how can I save Israel? Ω, and I am the least in my family."** (Judges 6:11,15)

What's the diagnosis? "I have self-diagnosed that I'm just trying to live a couple of more days." Diagnosis? "My family is the dumbest in the land. And in fact, of this dumb family, I happen to be the dumbest in the whole family. So, as you see, to sum up, I am probably the biggest dummy and nobody in the country. Move along." Well, at least he had a starting point.

BROKEN DOWN

Nehemiah did some pretty remarkable things for the Lord. But that process started with this:

> *They said to me, "Those who survived the exile and are back in the province are in great trouble and disgrace. <u>The wall of Jerusalem is broken down, and its gates have been burned with fire.</u>" When I heard these things, I sat down and wept. For some days I mourned and fasted and prayed before the God of heaven. (Nehemiah 1:3, 4)*

Diagnosis? "My people are in trouble." Diagnosis? "Stuff is broken down. It is burning down." Nehemiah sat and wept. He mourned and fasted even while he was seated in the chair of diagnosis. And sometimes we break down too.

"You've got cancer."

"You are broke."

"Your corporate reputation is in shambles."

"I'm leaving you."

"You can't make this team."

"This will never work. Try something else."

We hear these things, and they make us sit down and weep. It occurs to me that appropriate grieving and mourning within the diagnosis seat is a very important step in the transformation.

> **Godly men buried Stephen and mourned deeply for him.** (*Acts 8:2*)

Times of "deep mourning" come. Grieving bad situations is a process essential. Although grief comes, it must not stay. If we stay in the chair of diagnosis we become apathetic, paralyzed, or overcome. We have to keep moving down the line.

JUST A BIT

Sometimes the changes we need to make are miniscule. Four years away from an Olympic event, an Olympian might recognize she needs to shave four one-hundredths of a second off of her time. Small changes make big differences.

If you put into a search engine "small changes big difference," there will be more information than you can ever possibly read. You can find loads of testimonies on the power of making small adjustments such as making grocery lists, skipping gourmet coffee, getting up fifteen minutes earlier, packing a lunch, taking the stairs, and the like. If a pilot changes course by the most minuscule margin at embarkation how far removed will the plane be at disembarkation? It could easily be a thousand miles. Often small changes over time make the greatest differences.

BILLY CARTER

How can two siblings put their knees under the same dinner table, be raised by the same authority figures, and have the same basic mores, yet turn out so utterly different? I met Lillian Carter when I was twelve years old. (Yes, I'm rather ancient.) She raised four children. Jimmy became the thirty-ninth president of the United States. His only brother Billy became an alcoholic notorious for, among other things, his "Billy Beer." He ran for mayor of Plains, Georgia—about the population of a rural Walmart (maybe not that big!)—and lost. He died at fifty-one after a life of heavy drinking.

How can that happen? I don't know, but I have seen it many times in my decades of youth ministry. I surmise it could be that some just sit in the chair of diagnosis, while others move beyond it. The addict—I mean the heavy-duty, class-A, top-shelf addict—often knows he has to move to the next chair. But for many, the knowledge stops there:

"Man, I gotta change. Pass the pipe."

"One more line."

"Where is the box of doughnuts?"

"Last porn, I promise."

Diagnosis chair brings awareness of the need. Change is birthed and often buried in this chair.

So, now we know what the problem is. We process it according to how bad it is. We recognize, admit, and own the entire deal. Good. Now let's move into the second chair.

KEVIN

Kevin is a fifteen-year-old boy who wants to make the football team. We will follow his progress as he sits in each of the chairs of transformation. Here is the first part of his story:

"There is currently no way I will make it. I'm fairly athletic. I'm not the toughest kid in the world, but I'm not a punk either. I am sitting in chair number one. My diagnosis? I am weak, out of shape, and unproven."

SANDY

Sandy, a twenty-nine-year-old, was addicted to drugs. She finally decided she wanted change. It wasn't easy. She will share with us her path toward transformation as she sits in each chair. Here is the beginning of her story:

"I started on drugs about the same time as my friends, in my mid-teens. At first it was what they call 'recreational' or 'gateway' drugs like alcohol and pot. I was always good in school even with my addictions. It came easy to me. I progressed—regressed, that is—to cocaine, heroin, really I was game for anything. Chair number one was simple and ugly, simply ugly. I spent everything on drugs. I did unethical things to get money for the next high. I destroyed my life and my relationships."

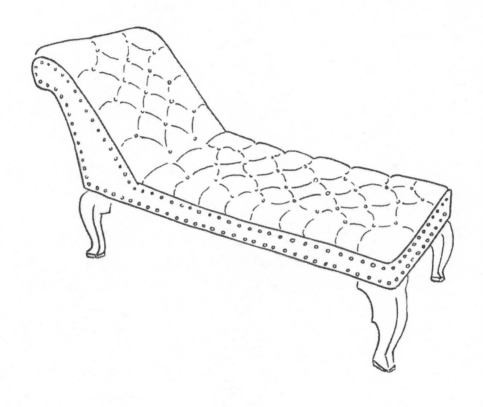

3

DREAM
CHAIR TWO

*Now Joseph had a dream, and when he told it to his
brothers they hated him even more.*
(Genesis 37:5 [ESV])

IN COLOR

A fifty-year-old friend of mine recently told me he literally said
to God, "Lord, confirm your will in my life through the process
of dreams." He told me he had rarely ever dreamed before that
prayer and had never dreamed in color. As he told me about how
God answered that prayer, I observed he was as excited as a little
kid. The details, the events, the colors of his dreams were childlike
in his description. It was very cool. And it was also kind of sad—
to have lived half a century without dreams. I dream just about
every night. Color-filled dreams. Exciting dreams. Frightening
dreams. Weird dreams. Heaven-sent and endorsed dreams. All
kinds of dreams.

What is really sad to me is the number of people who look in the mirror, look in the checkbook, look at the office cubicle, without ever

having holy daydreams. People may call unholy coveting a dream, but it is no dream:

"Look at his family tree. I could rock a suit too, if I had his genetics."

"Well, if I had been born into privilege, I might have something too."

"Of course he will get a promotion. He is the boss's nephew."

All of these statements are anti-dreams.

WHAT IFS

"What if...?" can be a bad question to ask. "What if...?" can be a good question to ask. We will see later the importance of planting explosive devices in the bad "what ifs" of our lives.

The good "what ifs" go like this:

"What if I *did* get myself in shape? How would I feel? What would it look like? How would it make a difference in my day-to-day?"

"What if I were reaching more people in the ministry for the right motives? What would this room look like? How would the excitement of the atmosphere change?"

"What if my marriage were passionate again? What if we felt like teenagers again and pushed through the monotony of the daily existence?"

"What if my business were booming? How could I affect change in the world?"

POWERFUL

Most references to dreaming in the Bible are very, very powerful. Punch the word *dream* into a Bible search engine, and there are almost a hundred hits, depending on the translation. Consider a handful:

> **He had a dream** *in which he saw a stairway resting on the earth, with its top reaching to heaven, and the angels of God were ascending and descending on it.* (Genesis 28:12)

> **The angel of God said to me** *in a dream* "Jacob." *I answered, "Here I am."* (Genesis 31:11)

> **He said to them, "Listen to this dream** *I had:* (Genesis 37:6)

> *When* **Gideon heard the dream** *and its interpretation, he bowed down and worshiped. He returned to the camp of Israel and called out, "Get up! The Lord has given the Midianite camp into your hands."* (Judges 7:15)

> *To these four young men God gave knowledge and understanding of all kinds of literature and learning. And* **Daniel could understand visions and dreams** *of all kinds.* (Daniel 1:17)

> *But after he had considered this, an angel <u>of the Lord appeared</u> to him in a dream and said, "Joseph son of David, do not be afraid to take Mary home as your wife, because what is conceived in her is from the Holy Spirit.* (Matthew 1:20)

> *"In the last days," God says, "<u>I will pour out my Spirit</u> on all people. Your sons and daughters will prophesy, your young men will see visions, <u>your old men will dream dreams</u>."* (Acts 2:17)

DAYDREAMING

There are dreams that come from God. There are dreams that happen while wide awake. In church. Driving. On break. These dreams shape our thoughts, behavior, and even destinies. They work in all kinds of ways. People who commit crimes and sins have often done so way before the physical act. Jesus validated this when he said:

> *But I tell you that anyone who looks at a woman lustfully has already committed adultery with her in his heart.* (Matthew 5:28)

PRODIGAL DREAMS

The Prodigal Son diagnosed himself precisely right. He was absolutely hungry and broke. In that process there is a flicker of a dream. Here it is:

> *But when he came to himself, he said, "How many of my father's hired servants have more than enough bread, but I perish here with hunger!"* (Luke 15:17 [ESV])

The guy saw bread in his head. He remembered his father's employee lounge as he walked his rebel road. He dreamed about the bread on that table. Hunger will do that to a person. The Bible says that a man's appetite drives him on (see Proverbs 16:26).

WALLS AND BIRTHDAYS

Nehemiah dreamed about rebuilding walls. He spent quite a while accurately diagnosing the situation. At some point he moved from despondency of what was into dreaming of what might be:

> *And I said to the king, "If it pleases the king, and if your servant has found favor in your sight, that you send me to Judah, to the city of my fathers' graves, <u>that I may rebuild it.</u>"* (Nehemiah 2:5 [ESV])

Gideon just dreamed about not being the star of his own funeral. God had to do a great sales job to push him past the ugly reality. In Judges 6:11, he was just trying to hide a little food from the enemy to live another day. He knew the end was near. At some point he opened the seal of his closed mind and let in some fresh air of possibility. *God says he will help me*, he thought. *Maybe I can "strike down the Midianites as one man."* Such a foreign idea. It had to take hold of him.

The dream had to take some roots. He allowed the dream to play just a few seconds at first. Then minutes. Then the dream began to linger. *Maybe I will see a few more birthdays and even secure some birthday candles for my people.*

BEYOND DREAMING

Lots and lots of great people started with simple dreams. The diagnosis is easy. The dream is fun. Then starts the work. If this is the last chair a person puts him- or herself in, well, it is the last chair in *fact*. There will be no change. The Bible speaks negatively about people who never put any feet to their dreams. Look at this list of negative characteristics that proceeds from not moving beyond dreaming:

> *Yet in like manner these people also, <u>relying on their dreams</u>, defile the flesh, reject authority, and blaspheme the glorious ones. (Jude 1:8 [ESV])*

Defiled, obstinate blasphemers. Wow. I don't want to make that list. So dreaming is indeed very important, but the train cannot stop here indefinitely. It has to keep moving.

NIKITA KOLOFF

While I was the pastor of a church in Huntington, West Virginia, I invited my friend Nikita Koloff, former world champion professional wrestler, to come execute a community wrestling outreach. We promoted the event in different ways in the community.

Nik rolled in one morning for a radio interview, parked his Cadillac outside the station, and walked toward me. I thought, "Man, that guy looks fit. That's how I would love to look in a dress shirt." I'm not saying I wanted to take the guy to a prom or anything awkward. This is just one alpha-male-wannabe looking at a professional wrestler alpha male thinking, *That is a change I need!* So when Koloff asked me to get him three appointments at a local YMCA gym for workouts and invited me to work out with him, I jumped at the free training.

He showed me his circuit routine—a process for change—and I adopted it. That was ten years ago. And I have indeed changed physically. I still have a lot more metamorphosing to do, but it started with a diagnosis and a dream. And then I put the dream into action. I moved beyond the dream.

TEN NOT FIVE

Nikita Koloff showed me five literal chairs to sit in while pushing heavy objects. He told me to do it regularly. I have done so for nearly a decade.

I have ten chairs to show you that can lead to your change. Diagnosis and Dream are only the first two. All ten of them are clutch stops along the way toward your transformation. The third chair is mandatory. It is the most important one. That is why we save it for the end of the book.

I could have just as easily used the metaphor of a train with stations. There can be ten stops, if you will, that occur in the transforming process. As each is outlined in front of you, I believe it will resonate with you, and you will relate to each one.

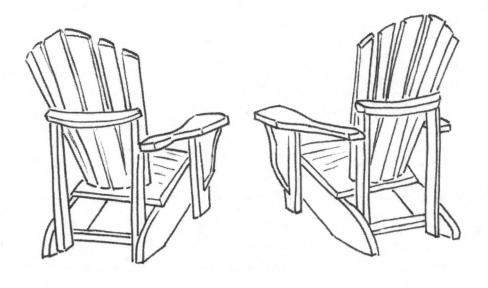

4

DIALOGUE
CHAIR FOUR (THREE COMES LATER)

Again, truly I tell you that if two of you on earth agree about anything they ask for, it will be done for them by my Father in heaven.
(Matthew 18:19)

ALMOST THE MOST

This chapter is about what to do after you diagnose what needs to change, the dream has been firmly established, and you have sat in the third chair—which is the most important one and which you will read about at the end of this book. Everything is like pedaling downhill after that.

This fourth chair is almost as important. It is the chair of prayer—hey, the Prayer Chair—the chair of dialogue with God. How can anything be more important than prayer? You will have to wait until the end of the book to find the answer.

THE CYCLE

I like the book of Judges. The Israelites of the Old Testament, the people of God, are both beautiful and ugly examples of God's people today. Judges is about cycle, vicious and contemporary cycle. Consider these verses (with my commentary in all caps after each one):

The Israelites did evil in the eyes of the Lord, and for seven years he gave them into the hands of the Midianites. Because the power of Midian was so oppressive, the Israelites prepared shelters for themselves in mountain clefts, caves and strongholds.

(DIAGNOSIS: HIDING FOR THEIR LIVES)

Whenever the Israelites planted their crops, the Midianites, Amalekites and other eastern peoples invaded the country. They camped on the land and ruined the crops all the way to Gaza and did not spare a living thing for Israel, neither sheep nor cattle nor donkeys.

(DIAGNOSES: RUINED PRODUCTIVITY and DESTROYED PROPERTY)

They came up with their livestock and their tents like swarms of locusts. It was impossible to count them or their camels; they invaded the land to ravage it.

(DIAGNOSIS: INVASION OF COUNTLESS ENEMIES)

Midian so impoverished the Israelites that they cried out to the Lord for help.

(DIALOGUE, Chair #4: CHANGE WILL HAPPEN NOW)

When the Israelites cried out to the Lord because of Midian, he sent them a prophet, who said, "This is what the Lord, the God of Israel, says:..." (Judges 6:1-8)

That cycle still happens in the lives of people today:

Fear→Loss of productivity→Stagnancy→Enemies of the soul→Destroyed opportunities→Fear. People that are addicted to pornography, for example, are often afraid of being discovered. They hide, delete and look over their shoulders. Useful projects are left undone. Stagnancy. Believers feel an overwhelming sense of guilt and Satan does not offer any solutions. He is the "accuser of the brethren" according to Scripture. Opportunities are missed as unworthiness washes over the addict. The addiction resumes and fear knocks again. The cycle continues.

Dialogue with God has a magnificent way of righting the course and beginning transformation.

DIALOGUE: DIAL DOWN

I used the term "dialogue" rather than prayer because, well, it starts with "D" and fits. And "dial" used to be a universal term for making a telephone call. In the olden days, we used telephones with wires that attached into the wall. And in the ancient times, there were phones attached to walls called "rotary phones," and we would dial one digit and wait a couple of seconds for the dial to return to base so we could dial another digit. The "dial in" principle as it relates to change applies.

> **Call to me and I will answer you and tell you great and unsearchable things you do not know.**
> *(Jeremiah 33:3)*

OUR JEWELL

My life, family, and ministry changed for the better on March 17, 2009, when I found a Jewell. Jewell Massey, a grandmother, called me about her teenaged granddaughter. We were not formally acquainted although I suspect we had spoken "hellos" in the church lobby over the years. She described the girl's plight. I said, "I am doing a fundraiser for our ministry on the twenty-second. Let us help you instead and give the profit to get her into a program. Your baby is in the ditch, and God can help her."

We raised a couple of thousand dollars for Jewell that night. I never dreamed the "sacrifice" of two thousand dollars would create a harvest exponentially greater for years to come.

In return for our donation, Miss Jewell took upon herself a divine calling, a burden, and a profoundly happy responsibility to coordinate an intense prayer ministry over every task this ministry team carries out for Jesus. At this writing there are at least fifty-five people—some I know and some I do not—who bathe our projects, meetings, and my family in intercession. I have supposed that about 85 percent of our requests to the prayer team have come to pass. Below are just a few examples.

FORT WAYNE

I missed the flight. It was a bad flight to miss. A missionary I had never met had solicited our services to raise money for his Mexico calling. I was scheduled to perform comedy at a missions banquet in Fort Wayne and receive an offering toward this mission. "There is no way you can get to Fort Wayne tonight. I have tried every way possible," said the very nice (really, very nice!) young man at Delta. He booked me on a late flight that would have made me completely miss the banquet. I would have only been there for an anti-climactic early Sunday service the following day. I called Jewell. I told her I was in a real crisis and requested immediate prayer. The team began to pray with urgency.

As I walked to the gate to wait for the late flight, an attendant I had seen several times before asked, "What is wrong with you? I thought you were a professional comedian."

"I am, but..." I explained the dilemma.

She clicked away at some keys and said, "How would you like to go to Fort Wayne right now and with a better seat?"

I know God heard the prayer team's cries just as certainly as I know my name is Rollin Joe Phillips. As memory serves, we raised around 5,600 dollars or more in monthly pledges at the banquet that night.

TRUST AND TRUCKS

After that experience, I began to trust the team with more and more requests. The requests got more personal, and they got bigger. I had a bone infection in my jaw. For preachers and comedians the mouth is the money-maker, so I put this on the team's prayer radar. They had dialogue with God. My jaw healed supernaturally quickly.

I got pretty bold one week and told Jewell I was tired of spending five thousand dollars per year on rental cars. The ancient Honda in my driveway was not trustworthy beyond the city limits. I was the rental company's favorite customer. (I joke that when I walked into the store, the employees handed me a balloon and a cookie.) "Have the team pray that I get a Honda Passport or a Chevy Silverado," I told her. One week later, someone not associated with the team put in my hand a set of keys to a Nissan Titan with twenty-two thousand miles. A significant thing about that moment is that I always asked for a Nissan car at the rental car company. I suppose I didn't even realize until I owned one that Nissan made a truck. So it's true that God is bigger than we think.

> **Now to him who is able to do immeasurably more than all we ask or imagine, according to his power that is at work within us**...(*Ephesians 3:20*)

MAYBE A PONY

I've done ministry for a very long time. And I've always known that prayer is important. Jesus Christ was God, and even he could not function and perform his calling without spending frequent time in dialogue with the Father. Paul spent frequent nights in prayer without sleeping. But when the above events and others like them began happening, I starkly realized that Ms. Jewell's crew was not a group of old people to pat on the heads, say, "Bless your hearts," and point to a corner room. "Go sit on the folding chairs, say some prayers, and enjoy some red punch. Next week bring some sugar cookies." Not at all! This was a team to move mountains.

This was a ministry to change the world and load the train with people for Heaven. I actually thought at one point, *Everything they pray for happens. Maybe I should ask for a hot tub and a pony.* But I didn't ask them to ask God for that. (Though he might have done it!) There are a great many more dramatic and quick answers to prayers. Other ministries I have introduced this template to have seen lives changed through their prayer teams. We are working on another project to document some of those transformations.

NO SUBCONTRACT

Although I rely heavily on this prayer team for the ongoing regular work of our ministry and my personal life, I can't subcontract them. Sometimes I have to get my own hands dirty in the work of intercession. I may not be "gifted"—as in having a supernatural empowerment from the Spirit—to pray as an intercessor, but I'm nonetheless required to find my "secret place," my spot, and have a dialogue with God regularly.

> *He who dwells __in the secret place__ of the Most High shall remain stable and fixed under the shadow of the Almighty [Whose power no foe can withstand].* (Psalm 91:1 [Amplified])

BIG CHECK

I was sharing the story of Jewell at Faholo, the same year I first delivered this sermon. A missionary in the back of a room of four hundred attendees later told me he whispered this prayer to the Lord (no subcontracting, *his* prayer): "Lord, I need a team like that." Immediately, the speaker (me) called him to the platform.

(Complete disclosure: I had to turn my microphone off and ask the worship leader for the guy's name.) I told the crowd Jason Forsman was a missionary to the public schools of Michigan and was at 30 percent of his fundraising goal. Jason shared this information with me the day before. I had not planned to share it with the crowd. As many things do, this just happened. "He needs to be at 60 percent by October, just three months away. We are not taking an offering. We are recruiting intercessors. There are four or six in the room (that was the sense I had from the Lord). He has a sweet wife in the back, pregnant with their first child. Give him your contact information after this service." Four of them did, and he was over-the-moon excited.

What I didn't know was the next day he was supposed to finalize an offer on a house he didn't think they could afford. His wife was ready to bring a baby home to a house and not the smoke-infested apartment complex they were living in. She had "mommy faith."

After I introduced him to the crowd that day, Jason went and taught a Bible study for the Michigan students at camp. When he went back to his room there was an envelope under his door with a check in it for five thousand dollars. FIVE THOUSAND DOLLARS! He was beyond excited. Two additional members of his new prayer team came forth that day, too. This chair is important!

JANE

Jane, a youth pastor, is living beneath her potential with very few kids attending her student ministry. She needs transformation:

"I'm not going to be falsely humble here. God's given me gifts and talents. I am a pretty spiritual person. There aren't very many students realizing this truth. They're not excited about me, the church, or the youth ministry; and worse, they're not enthused about God at all. In a church this size, in this kind of community, there should be at least fifty students who meet with us on a regular basis. Chair number one reveals that we're not even close to half of our minimum potential.

"I hear people say, 'Numbers don't matter.' But I know they do. They matter because every number represents a soul. And if numbers don't matter why is there a book in the Bible called Numbers? I dream about a room that's FULL. Full of students, full of energy, full of ideas, full of motivation, full of world-changers. We are anything but. I know this room doesn't glorify God the way it could. I love to dream about glorifying God with our quality, our enthusiasm, our passion, and all of those we convince about the goodness of the Lord. I want these students to 'taste and see that the Lord is good.' I dream about having every chair full.

"I sat in chair number three—the most important one by far—and I sprang from it like a rocket. I will describe that chair and why it launched me later on. I immediately found those 'crazy people' I used to avoid (and my students avoid simply because of their wardrobe!). There are four of them. Three of them are from the church I serve. The other is one of their friends. These people seem to walk to the beat of a different drummer, as the cliché goes. God speaks to them, they say, like he's in the room. I bought them coffee at Starbucks and shared the diagnosis. I was shocked by their enthusiasm. They just lit up. I thought, *This is the passion we've been missing*. So I signed them up. I guess I didn't really think it through because they pulled their chairs around me and prayed right there—in Starbucks! I was quite literally in chair number four. I didn't know it was going to be an immediate clock-in. (But I didn't even really care!) And I'm also praying like never before. Every day and with strategy. Dialogue chair means increasing my personal prayer life and it especially means recruiting those who love to intercede for a cause."

ROLANDO

Rolando, in talking with his wife, is woefully awakened to the fact that his marriage is stale. Over time he hopes to steer his marriage away from stale and straight into a place of sweet freshness:

"Something is missing. In a moment of perfectly secure honesty I asked my sweet wife, 'On a scale of one to ten—and ten is best— what number would you give our marriage?'

"And in sheer honesty she stated matter-of-factly, 'probably about a five.' When she said 'five' it was truly like one of those firehouse five alarm screams. It was like a sucker punch in the gut. Chair number one is an "oh my word!" I have guided this marriage to mediocrity. I want to move the needle from failing (50 percent is an F) to passing, and then to near perfection.

"I want to walk into my house and see my wife light up like she did when we were dating. I want to pursue her like I used to. I am dreaming about not taking her for granted and about doing special things together. I want to be her quiet hero. I dream about how this marriage can be. Seat number two is a little painful. I fight regret but pursue the vision.

"I have an 'odd' uncle. I go to church, but he *goes* to church. Like he never leaves it. When I get around him, I get kind of creeped out because he looks at me like he knows something about me. I told him—in strictest confidence (his sister is my mom, for Heaven's sake)—that I need to move the needle. He is praying with three of his 'warrior buddies,' as he calls them, whatever that means. But I guess it means something.

"I've also taken it upon myself to pray for my marriage from the moment I get on the connector each morning heading to work until the time I get off. It's about nine miles, and it's backed up sometimes, but I spend the entire time in dialogue with God. It's more than I was doing."

5

DIRECTION
CHAIR FIVE

Whether you turn to the right or to the left, your ears
will hear a voice behind you, saying, "This is the way;
walk in it."
(Isaiah 30:2)

"FRISBEE" GOLF

In the summer of 2011, I was introduced to "Frisbee" golf. To utter the sentence, "I'm going to go play Frisbee golf" didn't make me feel like an MMA fighter, to say the least. (Aficionados of the sport insist I call it "disc golf," so I will.) How difficult could it be to throw a disc at a basket? Well, there's no way I could look more afflicted trying to do something that sounded so simple.

There were about seven ministers playing that summer, as I remember. I threw it into the woods. I threw it three feet in front of me, behind me, everywhere but toward the basket. And the ministers beat me like I owed them money. I played four years of college basketball and ran a mile in four minutes forty-seven seconds when I was eighteen. But that day in the summer of 2011, I was a fat, unaccomplished disc golfer. I had more than broken pride, though. I had fun.

Disc golf is cheap and easy, light exercise. I was intrigued by the sport. I wanted to learn how to do it. So I talked to people and looked at videos. I bought some equipment and began to practice. I cut twelve or more strokes off my initial score on that course in one year, graduating from horrific to normally bad. However, it was a significant improvement. In other words, I dug out a plan and got some direction.

THE STEP DIRECTOR

When a person realizes what needs to be changed (Diagnosis), commits the improvement to holy imagination (Dream), does the most important thing (outlined later), and talks to the Creator about it (Dialogue), that individual then must sit in the next chair. He or she has to find a plan. That is Direction. And the plan should be simple. It's a Biblical principle to construct a plan:

> **A man's heart plans his way, But the Lord directs his steps**. (Proverbs 16:9 [New King James Version])

Yes, the Lord certainly directs our lives, which is crucial, but our planning the way is a good thing. A plan gives a person framework and direction, and it makes flowing with our 'step director' easier.

AUDIBLE

An audible is a wonderful thing in football. It usually comes at the line of scrimmage when the quarterback realizes the called play won't work with the defensive adjustment. He can see that a blitz is coming. The play they called in the huddle will surely result in a loss. He barks a change of plans. The line of scrimmage pops up one by one like ground hogs. They collect the information shouted. Sometimes the audible results in a touchdown, but it always begins with a called play. Dig out a plan. Call a play. The Lord can give you the audible. You were going to run a draw play. The screen is a better call. The big plan, however, never changes. Score. Succeed. Fulfill.

BUILD WITH PLANS

No great contractor walks out in a field and says, "Let's get started. All right, Fred, go into town and see if anyone knows anybody with shovels and one of those machine diggers. Tom, find out if there is anyone with a chainsaw who could cut these trees down and make us some boards. Hey, Ralph, look under my truck seat and see if there are any loose nails. We're going to build us a house this week, boys." Ridiculous. And it's ridiculous for us to make transformations without digging out simple plans first. I believe it's also silly to begin with the plan stage before one talks to the Lord about the diagnosed change needed. Get the information.

> *And whoever does not bear his cross and come after Me cannot be My disciple. For which of you, intending to build a tower, does not <u>sit down first and count the cost</u> whether he has enough to finish it— lest, after he has laid the foundation, and is not able to finish, all who see it begin to mock him.* (Luke 14:27-29 [NKJV])

FIGHT WITH STRATEGY

Losing teams show up on opening night and hand out the uniforms thirty minutes before the buzzer or whistle. "All right, boys, introduce yourselves to one another quickly. Let's see who plays what position. You boys talk out there. We don't have plays, so wing it." In history, that has probably happened. But history will find no championship teams with that mentality.

Arguably, the military is one entity within the government that runs more efficiently than others (with some exceptions, surely). The mission of military operations is always paramount. Brave soldiers may improvise, but they never get on a transporter just winging it. The men and women in uniform understand; a plan is crucial to carrying out a mission.

> *Or what king, going to make war against another king, does not sit down first and consider whether he is able with ten thousand to meet him who comes against him with twenty thousand? (Luke 14:31 [NKJV])*

"SIMPLY" IMPORTANT

So, is the change or changes that you need to make important enough to deserve your focused attention? In the transformation process, it's critical to get a plan. Here's a very vital component to the plan: simplicity. I read once that human beings vastly overestimate what they can accomplish in one year and dramatically underestimate what they can do in five years. Based on my experience, that is pretty true.

People have resolutions on January 1. "I'm going to lose fifty pounds, run a marathon (even though I've never run around the block), write a book, learn Latin, and build a Habitat for Humanity house this year."

On January 2, many say, as Jim Gaffigan recently quipped, "Well, I need to give my muscles time to breathe." And by the second week, the list of resolutions is a memory, because the task of accomplishing all of it within that year becomes overwhelming. If a person stretched that list out over half a decade, there's a real chance something great could happen. Regarding transformation, the rule is simple...simplicity. Jesus said his way isn't that complicated:

> *Then Jesus said, "Come to me, all of you who are weary and carry heavy burdens, and I will give you rest. Take my yoke upon you. Let me teach you, because I am humble and gentle at heart, and you will find rest for your souls. For my yoke is easy to bear, and the burden I give you is light." (Matthew 11:28-30 [New Living Translation])*

This plan isn't a goal. It's not a resolution. It is birthed from diagnosed need and filtered through dialing in the Spirit's power. This is done through prayer. So it needs to be a plan that is Spirit-birthed. Often those plans seem a little off at first:

"Go down and dunk a few times in the river, and you will be healed." (from 2 Kings 5)

"Go down to the water and catch a fish. The tax money will be there." (from Matthew 17:27)

"Leave this revival and go to a desert road that leads to Gaza." (from Acts 8)

People who are connected with God will walk with him, even when the plan sounds impossible. As we walk, we often hear some audibles within the plan:

> *Whether you turn to the right or to the left, your ears will hear a voice behind you, saying, "This is the way; walk in it." (Isaiah 30:21)*

Your Spirit-birthed plan might be as simple as these:

- Stop eating after seven pm.
- Buy your wife flowers once per week.
- Trust God with your tithes.
- Don't eat lunch on Wednesdays.
- Exercise while you watch *Jeopardy*.
- Call three people per week.

I don't want to be *too* simplistic. Some transformations may require a plan that looks bigger than these but that God will make 'easy and light' by his grace if you will trust him. The key is to get his plan and work that plan. As the old-timers used to say, "Plan your work, and work your plan."

Don't make the plan itself an idol like a lot of folks are prone to do. God is sacred. Plans themselves may or may not be sacred, but there is simply no replacement or equal to being led by Almighty God. The goal is obedient change.

THE TEACHER

One of the strangest things the disciples ever heard from Jesus had to be, "You will be better off when I leave." This is my paraphrase of John 16:7:

> **Nevertheless, I tell you the truth: <u>it is to your advantage</u> that I go away, for if I do not go away, the Helper will not come to you. But if I go, I will send him to you.** (ESV)

"Helper." The NIV calls him the "Advocate". Advocate means "a person who speaks or writes on behalf of a person or cause". That is what Jesus called the Holy Spirit. His job is to speak for and write (see 2 Timothy 3:16) on behalf of Jesus and the Kingdom of God. You, and the transformation you need, are important parts of God's Kingdom. And that Advocate can easily help you dig out the direction that will make the change happen. Here is a misunderstood—gloriously misunderstood—promise. It's a promise for you and the change you need:

> **As for you, the anointing you received from him remains in you, and you do not need anyone to teach you. But as <u>his anointing teaches you</u>**

***about all things** and as that anointing is real, not counterfeit—just as it has taught you, remain in him. (1 John 2:27)*

This "anointing" has within it shepherding imagery. Parasites would often attach to the wool of sheep and make their way into the sheep's ears, causing the animals to die. Shepherds would anoint the sheep's ears with oil, which kept the parasites from crawling into them. God anoints us in the same way, and that anointing gives instruction. It keeps the danger out of our heads. He knows the change you need to make. You know the change you need to make.

KEVIN

"My name is Kevin. Last year I watched the guys on game day. They always wore their jerseys and looked so great. The players were like the big deal on campus. I wanted to be part of a team. I dream of those bright Friday night lights and the crowd screaming. Chair number two was fun to sit in. I like to dream, but I also knew I needed to move beyond dreaming.

"I realize where I am and how far I have to go. I've sat in the most important chair, and now I'm ready for chair number four. So now I pray everyday about football, and I got my Nana and her little old granny group praying about it too. We even email each other about it. I couldn't believe Nana knew how to email. They aren't bugging me at all. I'm so happy someone cares about this—because I really, really care about it.

"I am 'putting some feet on my prayers,' as my Nana says. I am pretty shy, but I prayed for two days to work up the nerve to call the coach. I told him I wanted to play, and I asked him what I should be doing now to get ready. I'm glad I called, because I found out there are voluntary workouts at the field. I showed up twenty minutes early the first day to let the coach know how much this means to me. I was so sore the next day I could barely walk. But I keep going back. So that's one thing the coach suggested. Number two, I'm going to stop drinking tea and sodas. And number three, I checked out some books about great football players to get myself pumped. Those are three big things in my plan. That's the direction I dug out sitting in chair number five."

SANDY

"I went back and forth between the guilt of dreaming and the thrill of dreaming. With my personality, the dream itself is addictive. I watch people run in the park and wonder what it would feel like to be healthy enough to do that. I wonder how it would be to actually have a savings account and not spend everything and then steal even more. I sat in the second chair called Dream, and it was almost a guilty exercise for me. Even though the dream's still there, I have moved beyond chair number two.

"I'm in real trouble. I just got out of the most important chair. Now I'm in number four. It feels like my prayers have hit the ceiling. I'm not sure God will listen to an addict like me. I know a couple of religious fanatics who used to use with me. Somehow they are clean now, and I'm not, so I'm just desperate enough to ask them to pray for me. I know they will. I just hope they won't be pushy about it. I don't really know anyone else who prays. I try, but I'm better with needles than with prayers. So that's all I got.

"Out of the blue I met a lady in this support group thing (the judge makes me go—don't ask). She told me about a program called 'Teen Challenge,' and it sounded like something I need and everything I hate. After talking to her, I went out for lunch and actually saw a woman with a shirt on that said 'Teen Challenge,' so I asked her about it. I mean, I had never heard about it, and then two times in one day it's in my face, so I kind of had to. (My religious friends would go nuts!) It turned out that this lady is a director or some kind of big shot with the program. She sat down with me right there in the restaurant, and walked me through everything on her laptop. I'm so ready to live up to my potential that I'm going to do this thing. I know it'll take a year or more but as my new T.C. friend said, 'One year will buy you fifty.' One year will give me my life back. At the rate I'm going, I might not have fifty weeks. So, chair five? My direction? At least twelve months of Teen Challenge."

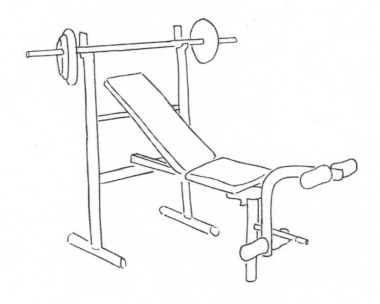

6

DISCIPLINE
CHAIR SIX

Do you see someone skilled in their work?
They will serve before kings;
they will not serve before officials of low rank.
(*Proverbs 22:29*)

I'M BORED

In this modern era of technology people often invite me into the front rooms of their lives. They "request" me to be their friend. What I find in those rooms I would never have found in the front porch days of my youth. When the neighbor invited you in for tea there wasn't all kinds of emotional drama everywhere—usually. (Actually, there was in my extended family, as I remember, but I digress. Focus, Phillips!) In my old age, I have found myself irritated by a phrase that has come into style. Youth seem to throw it around left and right, especially on social media: "I'm bored."

My standard stump speech about this expression (insert preacher voice) is, "A follower of Jesus should *never* be bored. There's always another prayer to pray, another chapter to read, another widow to help, another dollar to find for missions..." You get the idea. Boredom is a dangerous enemy. That old saying, "Boredom is the devil's workshop," is pretty much on the mark.

WHO'S IN CHARGE?

Maybe you're like me and need to change something. There are areas in my life that need to 1) change in form, appearance, or structure; metamorphose; 2) change in condition, nature, or character; convert; and 3) change into another substance; transmute. With all the available ways to make personal, career, academic, or professional changes, I can't see how anyone could possibly be bored. Don't get me wrong. Life can be a grind, and I would never suggest it should be a thrill a minute. People who have learned to overcome the enemy of boredom have found their address on a farm called Focus. They've learned to live with self-control, one of the beautiful and effective fruits of the Spirit:

> *But the fruit of the Spirit is love, joy, peace, forbearance, kindness, goodness, faithfulness, gentleness and self-control. Against such things is no law. (Galatians 5:22, 23)*

SLEEP TILL ONE

My last great memory of my family intact is from my freshman year of high school. We had just moved into an eighty-year-old farmhouse right on Lake of the Ozarks in southern Missouri. I made good friends and made the basketball team. Dad bought a boat, and we skied behind it. He bought me a two-hundred-twenty-five-dollar blue canoe that I fished in. My parents were still together.

The next summer, Dad wanted to work with another company and moved us to Florida. Life changed completely. He got mugged in an alley and was nearly killed. The job didn't go too well. We lived in an apartment above a garage and eventually moved into a small rental house. In the Ozarks, I had known all forty-eight people in my freshman class. When I started my sophomore year of high school in Florida, there were three thousand kids in three grades, but I didn't know even one.

No cable, no technology, no friends, no mission. Just me and a sweet dog named Rags. I had Rags going for me, and not much else. My mother was a very hard working woman. She was a great example to me but I foolishly was not led by it. I slept every day past noon because there was nothing to motivate me to do otherwise.

Or so I thought. In truth, there was everything to motivate me. (We will deal later in this book with the stupid stories we tell ourselves to hold ourselves back.) If I'd only known Christ and the truths he would later download to me (and that are found in this book). Yes, life was kind of rotten. Everything had changed. Mom was working, and things were just so off in our house. There wasn't much money. There wasn't much faith. However, I did have the same thing every other successful person has. I had the same 1,440 minutes every day. I also had my youth and energy. And I had desire.

LEADERSHIP?

There are lots of modern books and seminars on the subject of leadership. It's grown into a billion dollar industry over the last fifteen years. But not everyone is born to be a leader, and not everyone possesses the Spiritual and Biblical gift of leadership. If everyone were a leader, then there'd be too many coaches and no players on the field. However, there has to be bootstrap-pulling leadership in every person as it relates to *self*. If you have to make a real change in yourself, then it is time for big boy and big girl exercise of self-control leadership.

If you find yourself like I found myself in southwest Florida, going through the motions and waiting for the day to come to me, sit down in a chair called Discipline. You need to discipline and direct your time, your focus, your energy, and your money.

TELL TIME

I mean literally tell your time what to do. You have the same 1,440 minutes as Bill Gates, Michael Jordan, and Taylor Swift. You know what needs to change. It's been clearly diagnosed by now. You have dreamt about the change. You have done the most important thing (which we will deal with last). You have the prayer covering and program in place, your dialogue with the Lord. You have direction in a plan.

Now, tell your watch and calendar about your plan. Tell time how you are going to live and what direction you're going. One of my favorite verses from decades of youth ministry is this:

See then that ye walk circumspectly, not as fools, but as wise, <u>redeeming the time</u>, because the days are evil. Wherefore be ye not unwise, but understanding what the will of the Lord is. (Ephesians 5:15-17 [King James Version])

"Redeem" means to buy back; to recover. God says the days are evil. And all we have to do is pull up the headlines, and we see that fact in color. Evil. One method of pushing against that evil is to tell our time what to do. Ordered lives eliminate wasted lives which makes us potent weapons against wickedness. Tell the calendar what's going to happen with you. You may use your time to push away boredom or even to beat down bouts of depression. It is quite important in the process of transformation to direct your days.

JORDAN TEARS

I love Michael Jordan's story of the Chicago Bulls' defeat at the hands of the Detroit Pistons. He got on the bus after another beat-down that robbed the Bulls of the coveted championship. His teammates took it in stride. They were playing cards and listening to music, laughing. But Jordan wasn't laughing. He was furious. He knew they needed a change.

In *The Jordan Rules*, Sam Smith explains, "Just before he stepped from the post-game podium onto the golf courses of America, Jordan offered one thought: 'We have to do some things. We need to make some changes.'"

Michael Jordan decided to direct his days differently. He began to lift weights, which was not a commonly accepted practice in those days for basketball players. It was believed it would throw off the shot. Already a hard worker, when Michael began to discipline toward change, the rest would be history. He went on to become a six-time NBA champion. He made a change.

TELL MONEY

Changers tell their time and their money where it's going to go. They plan. But they're also flexible. And they direct their lives.

People who lose weight direct what goes into their mouths. People who have money have directed where they want it to go. Have you ever gotten to the end of the day and wondered where your time had gone? Have you ever had a little windfall gift—like a hundred-dollar bonus or gift from an aunt—and wondered, "What did I do with that money?" People who save money and transform their bottom lines have told their money where it's supposed to go.

Dave Ramsey uses a great illustration. He says when we begin to make these small directional changes in how we manage our money it's as though we go from walking on cement to walking on a moving sidewalk. He has made this catch phrase take hold: "Live like no one else so that you can live like no one else."

WORK: A FOUR-LETTERED WORD

After stopping at diagnosis, spending time on a dream, lingering at the vital yet-to-be-named "D," dialoguing with the Creator, and finding direction, you will find the business end of change (the last five chairs) involves a dirty, four-lettered word: *work*. Disciplined, focused, direct work. Each of these D's could be a book in itself, especially discipline. Scripture is full of examples and admonitions about work and discipline. Consider one here:

> ***All hard work brings a profit, but mere talk leads only to poverty.*** *(Proverbs 14:23)*

Talking about the diagnosis doesn't really solve, change, or transform a situation. To all the planners out there, planning never did much more than excite the planner and maybe those who buy into the plan. A plan has to have feet, however unpleasant it may seem at first. The Bible says it's not particularly pleasant to volunteer to be disciplined:

> ***No discipline seems pleasant at the time, but painful. Later on, however, it produces a harvest of righteousness and peace for those who have been trained by it.*** *(Hebrews 12:11)*

LAMINATED

I'm an odd duck. When I was a kid, I told everyone I wanted to be a filling station attendant. That's an obscure, outdated figure from history who would come to a human being's vehicle, fill up the tank, wash the windows, check the oil, and perform other small duties. I was completely mesmerized by the big wads of cash they carried in their gray uniforms. Mesmerized by the way they made change. That had to be the all-time coolest thing, making change at a gas pump.

Although a man, I still get mesmerized like that kid. But now it is from football games and seeing the coaches carry around complicated, multi-colored, and laminated game plans. (This is the new big wad of cash to me.) Coaches often cover their mouths with the plans as they speak into their headsets to the coordinators upstairs. I am fascinated with the laminated plan. Teams actually study the opponent's offense and defense to come up with the most effective strategies to counter those opposing strategies. Cool.

AUGUST SWEAT

The laminated, multi-colored, multi-faceted plan is not worth the office assistant's time in putting it together without brutal discipline under an August sun. Football comes down to the discipline of near-death experiences on practice fields. The sprints, the weight room, the film-studying, the dehydration, all happens well in advance of laminated game days. We dig out simple plans, but they mean nothing unless they are executed:

> *Do you not know that in a race all the runners run, but only one gets the prize? Run in such a way as to get the prize. Everyone who competes in the games goes into strict training. They do it to get a crown that will not last, but we do it to get a crown that will last forever. Therefore I do not run like someone running aimlessly; I do*

not fight like a boxer beating the air. No, I strike a blow to my body and make it my slave so that after I have preached to others, I myself will not be disqualified for the prize. (1 Corinthians 9:24-27)

POCKET EDITION

Many members of Congress have carried the Constitution of the United States of America—the plan created to run this country—with them in their pockets over the years. Senator Robert Byrd from West Virginia is one who comes to mind, as I remember having seen him use it. He often referred to it during debates.

Keeping a copy of your plan handy is not a bad idea, but an even better method of reference for your own prayed-over and dreamed-about transformation plan is to commit it to memory. Know the plan. Keep it simple and refer to it often. When you deviate from the plan (because you will deviate), get back on it quickly. No intelligent person, upon making a wrong turn into the seediest part of a city, says, "Too late. We'll just keep going until whenever." Smart people look for quick spots for U-turns and resume the GPS to their destinations.

NEHEMIAH

Nehemiah was just a cupbearer to the king. Learning the diagnosis that the walls of Jerusalem were broken down, he grieved. He wept. He dreamt. He sat in the third chair. He prayed and interceded. Then he developed a plan. He asked the king for permission to return and rebuild those walls. Boom. The plan was in motion. King Artaxerxes of Persia sent him to Judah as governor of the province. Mission: Rebuild the walls. This mission required discipline. Here are the details of that disciplined plan:

> *From that day on, half of my servants worked on construction, and half held the spears, shields, bows, and coats of mail. And the leaders stood behind the whole house of Judah, who were building on the wall. Those who carried burdens were loaded in such a way that each labored on the work with one hand and held his weapon with the other. And each of the builders had his sword strapped at his side while he built. The man who sounded the trumpet was beside me. And I said to the nobles and to the officials and to the rest of the people, "The work is great and widely spread, and we are separated on the wall, far from one another. In the place where you hear the sound of the trumpet, rally to us there. Our God will fight for us." (Nehemiah 4:16-20 [ESV])*

This plan serves as an example for the plans we need to develop.

GIDEON

Gideon was destined to do some exploits in his life. He would eventually lead Israel into forty years of peace. It required some prayer. He obviously was praying as he had a dialogue with a Lord's representative who many theologians think was an Old Testament appearance of Jesus. It required a plan and discipline. Sometimes the plan and discipline seems right. Sometimes it seems odd. Here is an example of Gideon's challenge:

> *That night the Lord said to him, "Take your father's bull, and the second bull seven years old, and pull down the altar of Baal that your father has, and cut down the Asherah that is beside it and build an altar to the Lord your God on the top of the stronghold here, with stones laid in due order. Then take the second bull and offer it as a burnt offering with the wood of the Asherah that you shall cut down." So Gideon took ten men of his servants and did as the Lord had told him. But because he was too afraid of his family and the men of the town to do it by day, he did it by night. (Judges 6:25-27 [ESV])*

This knocking down of the false god was a very big deal, and it was a very big part of the transformation. It didn't necessarily take that much effort to cut down. But it certainly took a great deal of courage.

ME

I once heard this quote: "The thing about life is that it's just so daily." That's the key to this sixth chair. *Daily* discipline. On a regular basis, I print a template of things I should accomplish weekly in this ministry. Here is an example of my daily, weekly, monthly, and bi-monthly goals and disciplines:

DAILY / WEEKLY / MONTHLY / BI-MONTHLY PLAN

DAILY TASKS
1. prayer time
2. Bible time
3. prayer with Cecilia
4. prayer with one child
5. read a great book

WEEKLY GOALS (of course this changes weekly)
1. writing goals (finish editing for example)
2. personnel goals (get an assistant on project)
3. details finished for important outreach

WEEKLY TASKS

SUNDAY
1. preach

MONDAY
2. travel
3. call minister(s)
4. call Mom
5. strength workout
6. calendar

TUESDAY
7. thank you notes
8. post office
9. bank
10. tithe
11. study
12. cardio workout
13. write
14. meet with administrative assistant
15. staff or other meeting
16. prayer team communiqué

WEDNESDAY
17. strength workout
18. off / Sabbath / rest

THURSDAY
19. write
20. home projects
21. study
22. cardio workout
23. Timothy project
    (encourage younger minister)
24. family meeting

FRIDAY
25. strength workout
26. administrative assistant
    communiqué

SATURDAY
27. travel
28. home projects
29. write
30. study
31. cardio workout
32. vehicle work
33. pack

MONTHLY TASKS
1. clean out garage
2. clean out emails
3. bills
4. balance checkbook
5. budget

BI-MONTHLY TASKS
1. supporter letter
2. communication with a mentor
3. prisoner communication
4. dry cleaner
5. blog work

Even in this paperless world, I have a printed copy of my plan I like to fold and keep in my front pocket. It's on my devices as well, but I like the feel of unfolding the paper and checking off the work as I go through it. I'm not a slave to the plan, and by the time you read these words you can guarantee the plan has already been adjusted. Stuff has been added and dropped, I am quite sure.

However, I don't just drop things from my plan because I don't want to do them. And I do grade myself weekly. Completing twenty-one of thirty-three tasks means I scored 64 percent. Not great. So I look at what I missed. If I missed "strength workout" half the time over six weeks, then I have solved the mystery of why I feel weak. A disciplined plan is a guide. It's a tool.

YOU

Pick a dreamed-about and prayed-over change you need in your life. When you feel secure about the simple plan you and the Lord have come up with to create change over time, here's some ancient advice from the prophet Habakkuk you can consider:

> ***And the Lord answered me: "Write the vision; make it plain on tablets, so he may run who reads it." (Habakkuk 2:2 [ESV])***

Run with the plan of God. Be disciplined. Be daily. Be changed.

7

DECLARATION
CHAIR SEVEN

It is written: "I believed; therefore I have spoken."
Since we have that same spirit of faith, we also believe
and therefore speak.
(2 Corinthians 4:13)

RIVER TIME

Several years ago, I was the pastor of a church in the mountains of
West Virginia. (It is a pretty fascinating story about how a guy living
in sunny Fort Lauderdale, Florida, ended up in the hills and hollers
of West Virginia, but one for another day.) The church doubled in
size during our three years there, and my outside speaking invita-
tions did as well.

The Lord began placing awareness of a diagnosis in my heart: I needed to be an evangelist. With a sweet congregation and four children
to feed, stepping out in faith as an evangelist was a rather terrifying
prospect. Evangelists primarily live from offerings and honorariums.
Imagine a sign that says *will preach for food.*   I had tried twelve years
earlier with abysmal results. There were big gaps in the calendar and
more than one check handed to me with *wish it could be more.* There's

a reason there were 2,500 employed evangelists in the 1980s but fewer than one hundred by some estimates today (in the denomination I serve). It took me a literal decade to climb out of the financial hole I'd created on the first go-round.

I equate my evangelistic decision to cutting grass with a riding mower on the side of a hill. Imagine gravity doing her work and the driver falling off the mower. And the tractor falling over the top of the driver with nearly decapitating consequences.

Sometime later the boss says, "Don't forget to cut that hill again."

"Uh, no thank you. I like my head. Find someone else."

That was essentially my ongoing conversation with God. So, for one year, I literally carried a little folding canvas Speed the Light (a youth missions organization) chair, my Bible, a notebook, pens, and my dog Dixie across the street from my house. I sat on the bank of the Ohio River at the place where the Big Sandy River joins it. I prayed fervently, rain or shine, for the direction of God for the change that was coming (or for the wisdom to know that no change was coming). I wrote, sat, cried, listened, and spent time with the Lord while the coal tugboats pushed back and forth along the great river.

I began to do something during that time which I have carried over until this moment. I stood at the end of my prayer time, stretched my hands up over that river, and made a series of declarations that have not changed in all these years.

MY FIRST FIVE

This might come across as self-serving or narcissistic, especially if you don't know this author personally. I'll take that risk and tell you my declarations, as well as an explanation of each.

#1. I am rich, famous, and successful. My family knows it, my friends see it, and even the very few enemies I have will live to see it.

> **Beat your plowshares into swords and your pruning hooks into spears. Let the weakling say, "I am strong!"** *(Joel 3:10)*

If the weak can declare to be strong, I believed letting the poor say, "I am rich," couldn't really hurt either. And if the Lord increases my notoriety, and I am making Jesus more famous, that may not be a bad thing either. Jesus has done quite well for two centuries without this human publicist. Nonetheless, I still declare number one.

#2. I am a creative preacher, writer, entrepreneur and comedian.

I knew at the time what the Lord had put in my heart for writing projects, but I was years from producing the first book, which is now in your hand. I was years from producing my first CD, DVD, or training seminar. But even though I was years from it, I knew it was already in me. Here was the idea:

> **As sorrowful, yet always rejoicing; as poor, yet making many rich; <u>as having nothing, yet possessing everything</u>.** *(2 Corinthians 6:10 [ESV])*

#3. I am an entrepreneur who produces outstanding growth resources for the Body of Christ.

I had in my heart this desire to help people for a long time. This declaration has, wrapped up in it, the idea of Romans 4:17:

The God who gives life to the dead and calls into being things that were not.

#4. I volunteer wherever I choose because I am successful.

I have often remembered this declaration over many years of giving away ministry. This has calibrated my expectation.

#5. And the reason I am successful is because I have committed my ways to the Lord and my plans succeed.

> ***Commit your way to the Lord, Trust also in Him, And He shall bring it to pass.*** *(Psalm 37:5 [NKJV])*

The more I've declared this, the more I've believed it.

FOOTBALL PROPHECY

Lots of football players (as well as other athletes) have made predictions that have come woefully short. In my hometown of Charlotte, North Carolina, one of our Panthers made the news recently. He didn't make it for his blocks and tackling. He made it for his words. He plays center and part-time prognosticator. He took out a full-page advertisement on his own accord in the *Charlotte*

Observer entitled: "Why the Carolina Panthers will win Super Bowl XLVII." Pretty bold stuff. It didn't happen the way he prognosticated. We do know his words stirred a great amount of publicity and locker room electricity. His coaches and teammates were right behind him.

There are some famous predictions that hit the mark, though, like Joe Namath's, all of those Super Bowls ago. The very first game to officially bear the name "Super Bowl" was played in January of 1969 in Miami (two years after the Kansas City game I mentioned at the beginning of the book). That game was regarded as one of the greatest upsets in American sports history. The New York Jets were big underdogs. The Baltimore Colts were heavy favorites. The underdogs won by a score of 16-7. Three days before the game, quarterback Joe Namath made an appearance at the Miami Touchdown Club. He guaranteed a victory and the Jets team backed it up. Whatever the score, words have more power than we probably will ever realize.

CREATION & CURSES

God is greater, bigger, and more powerful than any football player. And God "spoke" the world and universe into being. I wish I could speak into being a Lexus or lake house. There is no magic potion. We aren't witches or warlocks who pronounce spells. However, as believers, we have uncanny power to bless and curse. Unfortunately, we do both. And we shouldn't:

> **Out of the same mouth come praise and cursing. My brothers and sisters, this should not be.**
> *(James 3:10)*

When we speak negatively, we do a great disservice to the changes we need to be making. It's possible to torpedo our faith with our mouths. Our faith moves mountains. Faith is the victory that overcomes the world. It's a shield that we should pick up above all else to overcome the fire-filled darts Satan throws at us (see Ephesians 6:16) . Faith is what pleases God according to Hebrews 11:6. Faith is powerful. Fear is an anti-faith. It ruins dreams, lives, and souls. And fear ruins change.

SOAK & SATISFY

A person wanting to lose weight should massage faith into every aspect of that desired change. The businessman who knows he needs transformation must declare the power of God in that situation. The wife who knows deep down she is mean and who doesn't want to treat her family badly might have to, frequently and out of her mouth, declare God's power to give her the fruit of the Spirit of love, joy, kindness, and gentleness.

We believe the words our mouths speak. Even liars know the more they tell a lie, the more they believe it. If the principle works in the perverse aspects, how much more powerful is the positive working? When you declare over and over your faith in God's power over your change, your heart begins to line up. And there comes a holy payday:

> *From the fruit of their mouth a person's stomach is filled; with the harvest of their lips they are satisfied.* *(Proverbs 18:20)*

When I sat on that river so many years ago making these faith declarations over my life, I began to see myself producing outstanding growth resources for God's Kingdom. I am neither shocked nor surprised that people will want to be helped and can be helped by God's work in this formerly broke-down and beat-up kid.

PRACTICALLY

The out-of-shape dad diagnoses himself with poor health. He may want to declare:

"I can do all things through Christ."

"God is well able to give me a plan to become healthy."

"I am the temple of God's Spirit."

"He that has begun a good work in me will perform it until the day of Jesus Christ."

"I will get back to my fighting weight!"

"I am more powerful than I even realize."

I strongly recommend to everyone who desires a change to never agree with your enemy. This will sabotage your change. Here are some anti-declarations that are worse than having zero value; they are poisonous:

"I am always going to be out of shape."

"I don't have the will power to get healthy."

"What's the use?"

THE SECOND FIVE
#6. *My children all love God, and they are going to love him all the days of their lives.*

As of this writing, all four of my children are in ministry of some form. The oldest is a credentialed minister. What is better is that each of them maintains a genuine love relationship with God.

#7. *My kids' college education is already paid for, and some of those college-educated kids are going to come back and work with their father.*

We are still believing for the manifestation of this to be fulfilled in the lives of our children. We are trusting God that all loans will be paid off and that future loans will not be necessary. We have seen the Lord work some real miracles in the lives of our children.

#8. *My marriage is fruitful and prosperous like a fruitful vine.*

After making this faith-filled declaration, I noticed a change in my marriage. Conflicts in any close relationships are inevitable, but our conflicts began to have a lot more calendar between them. When a conflict arose, I immediately reacted to it as though it was a slop-covered pig in a fine china shop. It just seemed out of place.

#9. I am preaching the life-changing message of Jesus Christ to the nation and to the nations.

Remember, as I lifted my hands and spoke these words, I was preaching to about 135 people each Sunday morning in a sleepy West Virginia town. Since the inception of this practice of making these declarations, I have spoken to over one hundred thousand people in eighty churches, ninety organizations, six denominations, twenty-one states, and three countries.

#10. I am in the will of God.

I long to live my life in the will of God. As I sit in the chair of declaration—the chair of faith—and proclaim this, it does a few things. One is that it's a verbal reinforcement of the value of this life.

It makes me keenly sensitive to actions and decisions that violate the will of God.

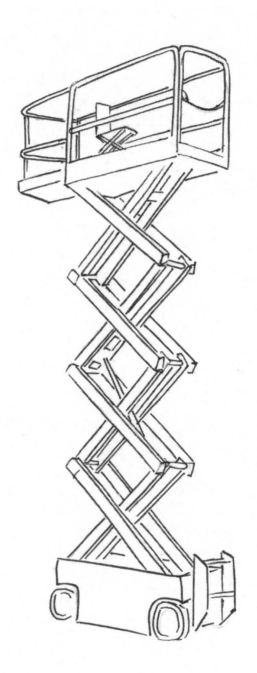

8

DETERMINATIVE
CHAIR EIGHT

*Do not despise these small beginnings, for the Lord
rejoices to see the work begin...*
(Zechariah 4:10 [NLT])

SCISSOR LIFT

Many football coaches utilize a contraption called a scissor lift. It's
an unusual-looking and, I'm quite sure, expensive device, the main
purpose of which is to elevate humans. It lifts them above a scene
for a different perspective. On a practice field, the coach sometimes
has a challenge seeing exactly how the players are missing a block.
Elevated coaches have completely different perspectives.

Similarly, in this transformation process the person desiring change
needs to elevate in order to evaluate. Is any progress being made? If
so, how much? And then you can determine the matrix from which
progress comes. On occasion, elevate yourself above the action and
look at the determinative. "A determining factor" is the definition
of determinative. It is the circumstance that settles or determines.
There are determining factors for nearly all changes required. That
old expression, "Can't see the forest for the trees," applies to change.

SCALE

For every change you need to make, there is an accompanying grid or system that will help you determine whether or not you are making progress toward that change. If a person needs to change his weight, the obvious marker is the scale. For a parent who is mean at home, the scale may be the number of times per week that unwanted behavior is demonstrated. This information might even be extracted in a moment of sheer honest feedback:

"How many days a week is Daddy mean around here?" that parent may ask.

"How many days are in a week, Daddy?" his child answers. "Seven? Yep, that's it. You are mean seven days, Dad."

After putting a plan into action for a few weeks, then stepping into the scissor lift and elevating himself, that father may find that he is harsh only every other day. That would be progress.

The bank balance is the grid for the young professional changing her financial situation. Number of pushups may be a determinative for Kevin. Number of students showing up in student ministry, Jane's measuring rod. The number of days Sandy stays clean and sober is a matrix. You get the idea. Now *get* the idea. Determinatives: simple units of measurement that let us know if we are on the right track.

SMALL MOVEMENT

In the great American cinematic classic movie *Dumb and Dumber*, there is a sequence in which the character Lloyd is trying to find some romance with the character Mary. Their hilarious dialogue goes like this:

Lloyd: What do you think the chances are of a guy like you and a girl like me ending up together? [*sic*]

Mary: Well, Lloyd, that's difficult to say. I mean, we don't really...

Lloyd: Hit me with it! Just give it to me straight! I came a long way just to see you, Mary. The least you can do is level with me. What are my chances?

Mary: Not good.

Lloyd: You mean, not good like one out of a hundred?

Mary: I'd say more like one out of a million.

[pause]

Lloyd: So you're telling me there's a chance?

There is a certain sense in this change process that we need to take notice of even a little flicker of improvement, just like "Dumb" Lloyd. In fact, we might need to intentionally celebrate every movement in the right direction. Any units of hope delivered, however miniscule:

"After three months I've only lost four pounds? Yes! I'm moving in the right direction."

"I've saved twenty-five dollars in seven months? Hey, that's way better than I did the seven months before! Keep it up, self."

Do not despise these small beginnings, for the Lord rejoices to see the work begin. *(Zechariah 4:10 [NLT])*

Small changes over time equal big transformation. The Grand Canyon is a great example of the effect of small change over time. It's 227 miles long, up to eighteen miles wide, and attains a depth of over a mile. The Colorado River established its course through the canyon (which was simply flat desert at the time) a long, long time ago. The Colorado River continued to slowly erode and form the canyon to its present-day configuration. A lifetime of observation of the erosion would have probably yielded few manifest changes. But over generations of time, that erosion produced one of the Seven Wonders of the World. We may not have generations to make our changes, but we have the rest of our lives. That means decades for some, years for others, and maybe weeks for still others. Some change is possible, regardless.

AUDIBLES

As the scissor lift raises you and me above the fight on the field, we might realize there is no progress toward our changes as of yet. In some instances, you might even find you've moved backwards. These moments are sentinel ones in the life of change. People have to do a couple of things right here. One, remember the Dream. Go back to that chair and push through discouragement and disillusionment. Second, return to the Direction chair and tweak the plan. Call an audible. We touched on the concept of an audible earlier in the book. Let's refresh the idea. An audible is a new offensive play called by the quarterback at the line of scrimmage to adjust to the defensive formation. If the defense coverage is set for a long pass, then a draw play might be called. Try calling an audible on occasion. Get yourself some quick wins. Third, go back to the chair of Dialogue. I mention it third, but it is so important. Talk to God. Tell him if you're discouraged. He knows it, anyway.

> *I pour out before him my complaint; before him I tell my trouble.* (Psalm 142:2)

WRITE IT DOWN

Regarding vision (always remember the Dream chair), a prophet had this instruction from Heaven:

> *And the Lord answered me and said, Write the vision and engrave it so plainly upon tablets that everyone who passes may [be able to] read [it easily and quickly] as he hastens by.* (Habakkuk 2:2 [Amp.])

We live in an age that has made it easier than ever to keep track of our progress. Dave Ramsey and hundreds of others have money tools available for our use. iPads, Macbooks, PCs, and cell phones make charting our progress as simple as a few clicks. There are apps for counting calories. (Do I use that? Perhaps I do. It is my scissor lift.) If you don't have access to digital tools, the old-fashioned pen and paper works fine. You can find a notebook and a pen for about a dollar. Chart the change. Celebrate the change. If the change is important enough to make, it's important enough to track.

RIGHT DREAM

On the scissor lift of determination there is, on occasion, a need to determine not only if this is the right plan, but also if this is even the right change. There are perverse changes people think they have to make.

"I'm too fat. That is my diagnosis. And I have a plan. Anorexia. But I'll switch it up with bulimia." The simple truth for thousands of young women and men is that they are not fat at all. Bad plan. Bad motivation for change.

Too many people think they need to change what's not broken. "I grew up poor, so I need money. I have a plan to work 85 hours a week. I will work this plan even if it kills me." Well, then, it might.

Fear can motivate people to change, and in some cases, marriages, families, and health are the collateral damage.

WINNERS NEVER

A winner never quits, and a quitter never wins. It's often true, at least true enough to motivate fifth graders on the recreational league basketball team. But as Seth Godin points out in his book *The Dip*, it's not always true. Nobody celebrates tenacious refusal to quit wetting the bed. We don't celebrate seventy-year-old men who said, "I got a job at McDonald's making burgers fifty-three years ago, and bless it, I ain't no quitter." Unhealthy obsessive changes are not worth pursuing as you evaluate. This issue really needs to be settled in the first and third chairs. Diagnose, "Do I really need this transformation? Is it a pride thing? Is it a narcissistic issue that really doesn't matter?"

WEED-EATER

When I was thirty-one, I had a job as a coach, athletic director, chaplain, and activity center director for a large private school. This portfolio made me busier than I could really keep up with. So it's odd that I was looking at a huge hill by the soccer field one day and thinking, *That looks horrible. Those weeds have to go.* I grabbed a coach and said, "Show up here Saturday. We are going to tackle that hill with a couple of weed eaters."

Saturday was hot. Really hot. Like, August in the Southeast hot. The machines were marginal at best in their effectiveness. We knocked a couple of weeds down that day. Really not more than a couple of weeds. The machines kept stopping. Gravity kept pulling us down. Cuts, scrapes, and flying and crawling critters all combined to make us mini Don Quixote – Cervantes' 1605 novel character who had wild visions of grandeur. Our enemy was not a windmill but a weedy, ugly, huge hillside. We quit.

The principal told me later, "Yeah, I'm glad you didn't get anything done. I need the roots of those plants to prevent erosion on that hill." That should have been thoroughly dissected in chair number one!

ZERO

For Gideon, there were a few numbers that helped him determine his success and failure. We could analyze the number twenty-two thousand. That's the number of soldiers who were scared of the enemy—quitters. Or we might look at the ten thousand soldiers who remained, not too scared to fight. There is a dramatic number of three hundred soldiers, whittled down from the ten thousand who fought, who gave God the glory for beating a mighty enemy with such few people. By this author's estimation, the number zero is the greatest determinative. According to Judges 6:6, there was great starvation of God's people. But they "cried out" (dialogued with the Creator). The winning number for the people came as zero. Zero days of starvation. Zero days of terror.

ONE

There are many ways we can determine the success of Nehemiah. The people of God were exiled and scattered. Because a man saw the need to make changes, sons, servants, and people found themselves in states of transformation. We sometimes get bored with genealogies in the Bible, however, the following list means something to me in the context of our subject. And there is great detail in this determinative. The total number of people revived to hear God's word again is 42,360. Many of those were "sons." This many sons: 2,172; 372; 652; 2,818; 1,254; 845; 760; 648; 628; 2,322; 667; 2,067; 655; 98; 328; 324; 112; 95; 188; 128; 42; 743; 621; 122; 123; 52; 1,254; 320; 345; 721; 3,930; 973; 1,052; 1,247; 1,017; 74; 148; 138. Nehemiah chapter seven and eight describes a holy celebration of renewal. Every number represents a transformed son that was part of the renewal. These sons were captives reassembled in ruins rebuilt. For most, it also represents transformed wives, children, and homes of those sons. These numbers occurred because Nehemiah saw something that needed to change. Wow. Amazing.

They had no horses, camels, singers, donkeys, nor money before Nehemiah began the change process. And after? Well, the numbers (see Nehemiah 7:66 and following) speak to his effectiveness:

- 245 singers, male and female;
- 736 horses;
- 245 mules;
- 435 camels;
- 6,720 donkeys;
- 41,000 darics of gold;
- 50 basins;
- 97 priests' garments and
- 4,700 minas of silver;

That's a lot of stuff and a lot of numbers. The most impressive number to me, however, is *one*. They started with no wall to protect the people. As Nehemiah determined if the plan was working, he needed to do nothing more than look at the wall. One wall. As the wall went up, so did the possibility of living a secure life with God's reassembled and renewed people.

PRODIGAL PARTY PACK

Regarding the "prodigal son," here are some interesting numbers. One fattened calf. One special robe. One father's hug. Two shoes. One kiss from Pop. One big, fat party was the measuring rod for a broken down, wasted, starving, lost son. In fact, as he smelled that veal being prepared, he knew. Change was on the way.

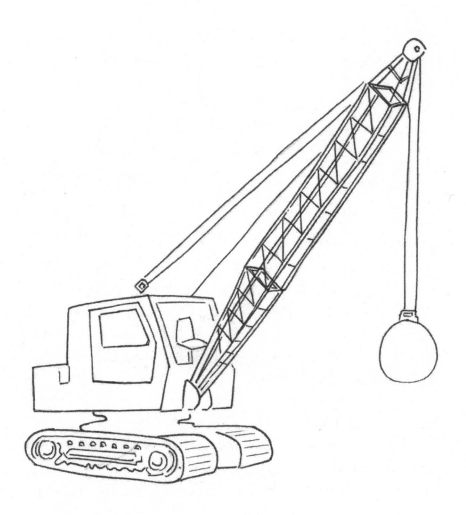

9

DEMOLITION
CHAIR NINE

We demolish arguments and every pretension that sets itself up against the knowledge of God, and we take captive every thought to make it obedient to Christ.
(2 Corinthians 10:5)

PICK A TIME

Pick one, because it's coming. At some point in the process of trying to change, something prickly will attach itself to you. It's called an excuse. Often it brings with it lots of other attackers. And as my grandfather reminded me as a child, everyone has them, and they all stink. Excuses are your enemy.

We discussed in the previous chapter that some imagined needs for change are better left ignored. That's not a license to quit on real changes that you must make. "If you don't lose weight, you will die," your doctor tells you. Well, that is not one of those "If it ain't broke, don't fix it" moments. When it is broke, fix it! Like blood pressure that needs to come down. Like driving all of your family away with your horrible attitude. Like tendencies to slide into debilitating

depressive moments that paralyze any hint of efficiency. Stinking excuses will attack genuinely-needed change.

BULLDOZER

"Johnson Family, are you ready to see your house? Bus driver, move
that bus!" Ty Pennington, host of *Extreme Makeover Home Edition*,
made these words famous. The camera zooms in on the family as
they see their renovated home for the first time. The more reserved
people put their hands over their mouths or fan their tears away.
People like me throw both hands out, scream, start punching people, hugging people, screaming "shut up" and some other, incoher-
ent things. Most of those renovations start with a bulldozer. The
existing has to be destroyed before the transformation can happen.
One of the absolutes in change is the demolition of the excuse. The
dilapidated home fills a need, but it isn't optimum. Likewise, excuses
scratch a weak psychological itch, but they are not conducive to a
wonderfully fulfilling destiny.

> *We demolish arguments and every pretension
> that sets itself up against the knowledge of God,
> and we take captive every thought to make it obe-
> dient to Christ.* (2 Corinthians 10:5)

FIRST & LAST

The excuses attack at the beginning, during challenges, and right
before victory. Procrastination, another enemy, has prevented the
needed change for so long because of these attacking excuses.
(Remember when I said excuses bring with them other attackers?)
The excuse is like a three-hundred-sixty-pound offensive lineman

in front of us saying, "Don't even think you are going to get around me."

When the diagnosis moved into dreaming, you addressed the most important chair and progress began. The dialogue got intense, pure, and sweet. Then, boom—a plan, a direction, was dug out. Discipline came easier than you thought. Regular declaration began, like miracles, to grow into expectations. You determined that there has been some progress!

Then, so often, a wall presents itself. It hits you right in the face. Knocks you back. Maybe an unforeseen financial emergency wipes out all good progress. A wedding reception breaks you down with its magnificent delicacies, and you don't just fall off the wagon, you trampoline off the wagon and down a jagged cliff. The very thing that kept you from moving through the chairs of change in the first place is back: Mr. Excuse.

SMELLY

I have made a few hundred hospital calls in my life. When I walk down a hall, I have often diagnosed various hospital smells—"Hmm, that's bad food. That's antiseptic. That's cleaner. That's...uh oh." Like diagnosing smells, these excuses can be smelled out as well. Let's smell a few:

"I didn't have the right parents. If I had the silver spoon experience John had, I might be further along, too."

"My parents made it tougher than anybody else's."

"It's my genes. Have you seen my family? We're all this way. Genetic fairies sabotaged me from day one. Whaddaya gonna do?"

"This is just the way I am. Take it or leave it. The concrete is hard, and I ain't changing."

"I subscribe to Murphy's Law. Whatever can go wrong will go wrong. It has always been that way for me."

NO LEGS

My job lets me meet thousands of kids and adults from all over the country. At national conventions I hear, "Pastor Joe, it's me! How are you? I saw you last year! Remember?" I speak or do comedy at about four to six big camps per summer as well as conventions and conferences, so I don't always know which events they saw me at last, but I always love to see them.

Sometimes, because of social media, some ministry continues beyond a particular event. A few years ago, a very troubled young lady from the Midwest continued the dialogue after the event during which we met. She had some image issues, some loss issues, some trust issues. I did my best to encourage her and give her hope. I tried timely Scriptures. She always retorted with an excuse about why she couldn't move out of her morbid introspection.

Exasperated one day, this was all the advice I had for her: "Google Australian preacher with no legs and arms." I couldn't think of his name at the time, which in fact is Nick Vujicic. I wanted her to see the story of this man born without legs or arms, but born again in

Christ with an electric attitude of positivity. This kind of human being exists on this earth. He has every reason to build excuse monuments, and the fact that he destroys the excuses makes him a transformation salesman for others.

THE WANDAS

There are other transformation salespeople out there. People like Wanda Grimes in Columbus, Georgia, born with a degenerative disease. Physically, she has never been "right." When I see her she flies down the church aisle to meet me in her motorized wheelchair, and she hugs me with her good arm. This thin-haired Wonder Woman tells me, despite her communication challenges, about great things God is doing in her life. She tells me that she's regularly going to see some of the most hardened criminals in prison and handing them some Bibles and some hope. "They stopped people (apparently a warden or other leader implemented new policy) from going into the jails, but they don't tell me to stop," she says. I wouldn't tell her to stop either! In the presence of people like this, I have no excuses.

Like the lady I met in Roanoke, Virginia: Linda. Her pastor told me before our visit that Linda could hardly move due to pain. She was fairly young, only in her early sixties. I went in to visit her. She was in lots of pain, and it was consistent. But she was sitting up in a chair, a bright light in that room. Her pastor shared that during a very challenging time in the ministry, her prayers were lifesavers. He is convinced of this.

I asked her if I could pray for her, and as I did, I saw a picture of a long corridor, like a corridor in a Sam's or Costco. I saw framed photographs like 'Employee of the Month' photos lining the corridor. Hers was among them. I said, "Dear Lady, I saw a picture. I believe in Heaven you have a superstar status, even if not many people here know about the mountains you are moving." (I typed these words about Linda not knowing that a month after our visit, the Lord had called her home to Heaven. Wow. What a picture the Lord gave me about a person who had no excuses.)

KEVIN

"I have a great plan. And I'm doing a few things to discipline myself—chair number six—within the plan. Like, I go to bed before midnight every night now, so I can be rested for practice. I almost never did that before. I don't get worked up playing video games anymore before I hit the sack. I drink some milk and read, say my prayers, and then go to sleep. I go to the voluntary workouts even when I'm sore because my dad says there's good pain and bad pain. I don't have an injury, which is bad pain; I have good pain from making progress. I quit caffeine and sugar. I'm disciplining myself, and these three things make a huge difference; more than I even imagined they would.

"Chair number seven isn't that easy for me. I kinda tend to bend negatively. I think 'positive' people are mostly fake, and I can't stand fakes. But I've disciplined myself to write down every negative thing I say. I figured when I started it would be like a couple per day. It started out like twenty-five complaints and curses a day. I realized how often I was saying stupid things like 'I'm never gonna make the team,' 'I'm so slow,' and 'They are gonna kill me.' (Pastor Jon says cursing is worse than cussing.) And I realized I can't just quit the bad talk; I have to start the good. So I say, 'I can do all things through

Christ who strengthens me' about ten times per day now. I say it every time I lift weights. And when I want to complain, I say other stuff instead, like, 'God is big enough to make me big enough,' and, 'I'm going to play football for Northside High School.' I don't know if it's making a difference, but I am starting to believe some of it. And Mom says I'm acting different—whatever that means.

"I got no problem with chair number eight—determining the measuring units. For players, it's always the clock. How fast is my time in the forty-yard dash? At my first voluntary workout, I am ashamed to say, it was five and a half seconds. I have carved off three-tenths of a second from that time. I could only bench 105 pounds. Now I'm at 165. Still terrible, but Barney, the strength guy, said it was a big improvement. My clothes fit a little looser, but I've gained some weight. Weird. Barney said it's because muscle weighs more than fat, so that's cool.

"I've made a lot of excuses over my life: 'Nobody ever taught me how to play football the right way as a kid.' 'My family gave me bad genes.' 'I never got pushed to go to football camp.' Those are stupid excuses, and I'm sick of renting space in my head to them."

SANDY
"Chair number six makes me want to cuss authentic swear words. I am inherently *not* disciplined. That's why I'm an addict. The directors took my smokes on day one. Are you kidding me? With all the junk in my life, cigarettes should be considered an organic health food. Prescribed nerve pills will help me with the jitters. Oh, wait, they took those too! When they told me I couldn't have caffeine and soda, I thought I had joined a cult. I was ready to walk out before somebody emerged from a shadow and made me put on blue Nikes,

drink Kool-Aid, and wait for the spaceships to come. I even had my bag packed, but as I turned toward the door I remembered a dream I did not have before coming here. I want to be a clean and sober mom one day. I want to hold a baby without being jittery. I'd come too far to quit. So I unpacked all my stuff and sat in discipline, ready to jump through all their cultic hoops.

"Declarations of faith? Huh? Quitting my cigarettes, narcotics, and sodas could not have been stranger than this chair, number seven. I am as used to cussing and cursing as I am getting high. It's easier, and it's free. I've always cursed my life: 'My life is *******,' 'I hate myself,' and 'Why would anyone take a chance on a ******** like me?' That, and way worse, was always standard conversation. It's been the default setting of my mouth. The good Lord knows I'm trying, though. I asked the staff here to give me some positive things to say. These are the declarations they gave me:

#1 *I am the temple of the Holy Spirit of God who lives inside of me.*
#2 *I am the handmaiden of the Lord.*
#3 *I am God's workmanship, and He created me to do good work.*
#4 *He that began a good work in me will perfect it until the day of Christ Jesus.*
#5 *He is able to keep me from falling and present me faultless before his throne of grace.*
#6 *Greater is the one in me than the one that is in the world.*
#7 *I will not be mastered by anything.*
#8 *I am a bondservant of Jesus Christ.*

So I say them everyday, and they tell me that one day, if I say them long enough, I will start believing and acting out what I am saying.

"My friend in here is a 'third year' (hope they don't think I'm staying three!), and he made me some laminated cards. I carried them everywhere for a while and quoted them all the time, even when I was drifting off to sleep. I don't need them anymore, because they are in my heart. I still quote them constantly.

"Chair number eight is simple for me. Needles and calendars. No subjectives whatsoever. No needles is my scale. Zero. Zero pills, bag, pipes, and dollars to dealers. Zero. And more days on the calendar is my measuring stick, my matrix, the determinant. I want there to be no drug paraphernalia in my life whatsoever, and I want there to be so much calendar between now and my last high that it feels like an ancient history class.

"Excuses are boring to me. It seems like I had more excuses than I have had needles in my life. So many I can't keep track of them. I'm making progress, so I don't even want to disrespect it by giving credibility to those lies now. Everybody has problems. Everyone has a past. Achievers overcome them. For so many years, I framed the problems and hung them on the walls of my mind. Every new high or binge was a salute to those hanging excuses. I now choose to demolish those lies daily. If I've learned anything in here, I've learned this: We have an enemy, and he is a stinking liar."

10

DISPLAY
CHAIR TEN

And we all, who with unveiled faces contemplate the Lord's glory, are being transformed into his image with ever-increasing glory, which comes from the Lord, who is the Spirit.
(*2 Corinthians 3:18*)

BULLETIN BOARD

One of the dumbest things an athlete can do before the big game is to denigrate the opponent. Even if, in the deepest part of his heart, he believes the opposition to be in every way inferior, wisdom keeps that insight inside and undisclosed. Over my lifetime, I have witnessed savvy coaches take these stupid words and post them on the bulletin boards. I've seen a coach take some cocky athlete's harsh assessment of another and make frequent rallying references to it to motivate the criticized athlete. He puts it on the athlete's locker. He may even blow up the words and prominently display them above the door leading to the practice field. The desired effect is for the athletes to know what the enemy thinks of them. Coaches want athletes to work hard to make sure the opposition has had a wrong prophecy.

MICHAEL PHELPS

Tyler Clary was Michael Phelps' teammate on the 2012 Olympic Swim team in London. When baited by a journalist, he said Phelps' natural talent, not his work ethic, caused him to excel. He called his teammate lazy. A journalist further insulted Phelps by calling a losing gymnast "Sunday's Michael Phelps." And after Phelps was slapped down early in the 2012 Olympics, finishing fourth in the 400-meter individual relay, many began writing him off as a has-been.

But Michael Phelps used those negative comments as fuel. He finished the 2012 Summer Olympics as the most decorated athlete to compete in the Olympic Games. Ever. The world-class swimmer finished his Olympic career with eighteen gold medals and a total of twenty-two medals overall. There is a good chance no one will ever replicate this success.

Champions use the negative words of their opponents as "bulletin board fodder." Of course this philosophy should be balanced. There is danger of becoming so obsessed with negative words that one allows them to become psychological quicksand or even idols. A healthy perspective is what the Psalmist penned thousands of years ago:

> *Give me a sign of your goodness, that my enemies may see it and be put to shame, for you, Lord, have helped me and comforted me. (Psalm 86:17)*

YOUR ENEMY

The enemy of your soul is, ultimately, the "Devil," "Satan," "Beelzebub," "Big Red," or any other name you might want to call him. He is constantly telling on us. The oldest book of the Bible, Job, indicates in the first chapter that the enemy walks back and forth on the earth collecting dirt on people (Job 1:7-9). The last book in the Bible, Revelation, says there is a day coming when he will get what is due him:

> **Then I heard a loud voice in heaven say: "Now have come the salvation and the power and the kingdom of our God, and the authority of his Messiah. For the Accuser of our brothers and sisters, who accuses them before our God day and night, has been hurled down.** (*Revelation 12:10*)

Notice Satan is called the "accuser of the brethren." When "accuser" is used in the Bible, it refers to one who brings a charge against another.

HELL MEDIA

In Hell, the barrage of bad press is about our rotten sin. Jesus Christ, the Son of God, dealt with this on the cross. He became sin on our behalf so that we might become the righteousness of God. In essence, when he shouted "*Tetelesti!*" (literally, "It is finished,"—"This debt is paid,") he shut Satan's mouth about that stupidity.

Because of what Jesus Christ did, our enemy has no legal right to blame us. Jesus paid for our freedom. But sometimes we Christians still agree with Hell's press releases about us:

> *The heart is deceitful above all things, and it is*
> *exceedingly perverse and corrupt and severely,*
> *mortally sick! Who can know it [perceive, un-*
> *derstand, be acquainted with his own heart and*
> *mind]? (Jeremiah 17:9 [Amp.])*

Our perverse hearts sometimes allow us to believe Satan's lies, but we do *not* have to. Jesus won.

Jesus was perfect. PERFECT! He never had a bad thought, said a bad word, or did a bad thing. Yet he was "accused" of being illegitimate. Accused of being a womanizer, a drunk, demon-possessed. Accusation is an old trick. So when Satan cannot convince God of how treacherous we are in our sin, he insults and accuses us instead.

Bullies, liars, gossips, discouragers, and all the other wet blankets aren't really the problem. The Bible reveals to us the real problem:

> *Our struggle is not against flesh and blood,*
> *but against the rulers, against the authorities,*
> *against the powers of this dark world and against*
> *the spiritual forces of evil in the heavenly realms.*
> *(Ephesians 6:12)*

SOME HELL HEADLINES

Here are some of the headlines coming out of Hell:

Johnson, Destined for Obesity

Late for Life

Won't Make Any Team

Smith, Still Below Potential
Kids Won't Know God
Customers Won't Buy
Fake and They All Know It
Marriage Still Stuck

I believe one of the best ways to shut the mouths of our critics and enemies is to simply win. Get a bunch of little wins under the belt on the way to the big win. When you travel from Diagnosis to Demolition, inevitably you will be prominently seated in the final chair of Display. You will display and demonstrate the change. You don't need a T-shirt that reads, "I've changed." You don't need a public relations firm to release the news. People will simply know. Satan will know. You will know! And God, who knew all the time, will know and see the difference.

> *Show me a sign of [Your evident] goodwill and favor, that those who hate me may see it and be put to shame, because You, Lord, [will show Your approval of me when You] help and comfort me.*
> (Psalm 86:17 [Amplified])

They will see the help and the comfort of Heaven through your change.

PARADE

Parade organizers often display the parade king and queen prominently in the back of a truck or on top of a car seat in a convertible. Parade attendees line up and applaud for the king and queen. That's the image I have of you at the end of your change. The "I'm on Time" King riding in the convertible. The "I Climb Steps Without Getting Out of Breath" Queen waving at the crowd. How wonderful will it be to be transformed from always being scared to always trusting God? This is not an arrogant parade.

You can be a star:

> *So that you may become blameless and pure, children of God without fault in a warped and crooked generation. Then <u>you will shine among them like stars</u> in the sky.* (Philippians 2:15)

You can be confident:

> *The fruit of that righteousness will be peace; its effect will be quietness and confidence forever.* (Isaiah 32:17)

Quietly and confidently display the great change, that great transformation before the Lord.

A WALL

From broken down to built up. From ruined to results. Out of big heaps came big help. Broken and ruined heaps of rocks existed before Nehemiah received the diagnosis. Like entering the Appalachian Trail, Nehemiah began the transformation trail. At the end, it must have been gratifying to see, demonstrated before the entire world, his great change. What a display:

So the wall was completed on the twenty-fifth of Elul, in fifty-two days. When all our enemies heard about this, all the surrounding nations were afraid and lost their self-confidence, because they realized that this work had been done with the help of our God. (Nehemiah 6:15, 16)

A FAMILY

F. Scott Fitzgerald's American classic, *The Great Gatsby*, has inspired many movie versions attempting to capture the grandeur of the literature. In the latest film version with Leonardo DiCaprio, we find the main character alone at the end of his life. He had been well known for throwing decadent 1920's parties, attended by throngs of his contemporaries. But there is literally one person at his funeral. That could certainly have been the end for the Prodigal Son of the New Testament. But his display was so much better. He received— or rather, he was received by—his father. His relationships were restored (with the exception of one brother with a crummy attitude). Rather than a funeral, he received a party:

But the father said to his servants, "Bring quickly the best robe, and put it on him, and put a ring on his hand, and shoes on his feet. And bring the fattened calf and kill it, and let us eat and celebrate. For this my son was dead, and is alive again; he was lost, and is found." And they began to celebrate. It was fitting to celebrate and be glad, for this your brother was dead, and is alive; he was lost, and is found." (Luke 15:22-24, 32 [ESV])

RESCUED WORLD

Gideon was going to die. Everyone he knew was going to die. He needed a change but had resigned himself to a script he presumed had already been written. But when the spark of possibility entered his mind and then exploded into a full-blown dream, he got busy. Gideon wasn't perfect by any means, and he certainly did some stupid things later in life. However, change happened:

> *Then the men of Israel said to Gideon, "Rule over us, you and your son and your grandson also, for <u>you have saved us</u> from the hand of Midian." Gideon said to them, "I will not rule over you, and my son will not rule over you; the Lord will rule over you." (Judges 8:22, 23 [ESV])*

FLIP THE SCRIPT

Let's flip some of Hell's headlines. Imagine the headlines becoming dramatically different because of your transformations. How about this for contrast?:

Johnson, Destined for Obesity
transformed to
JOHNSON, 80 LBS DOWN AND COUNTING

Late for Life
to
ALWAYS ON TIME

Won't Make Any Team

to

STARTER!

Smith, Still Below Potential

to

SMITH, OVER-ACHIEVER, ODDS BEATER

Kids Won't Know God

to

EVERYONE WALKING WITH GOD

Customers Won't Buy

to

FLYING OFF SHELVES

Fake and Everyone Knows It

to

GENUINE ARTICLE

Marriage Still Stuck

to

PROSPEROUS MARRIAGE

All things are possible. All things are possible. All things are possible. You can display and demonstrate a magnificent transformation. It is possible.

JANE

"From my times of dialogue in chair number four, I have already made these simple adjustments. I asked mature students to consider this—with their parent's permission: a weekly consecrated fast, Wednesdays from sunup until four pm. We break it every week with communion and then pizza or whatever.

"I am more intentionally focused on relationships than ever before. I received my pastor's permission to have an artistic student paint a huge, three-month calendar on the wall in the youth sanctuary. The blank spaces are filled with artistic reminders of student recitals, games, debates, and so on. Multi colored sticky notes are all over the thing, and pictures, too. The kids show up early now to youth group meetings and find their dates and pictures. I love all that stuff, anyway, and I am going to attend as many events as possible.

"Also, I am determined to improve my speaking style. I am an OK speaker, but I think I bore kids. And as one great veteran youth worker said decades ago, 'It is a sin to bore kids with the Gospel.' I'm being mentored in a focused speaking improvement program.

"So prayer is ratcheted up, relationships are more intentional than ever, and the quality of my public ministry is already improving. I'm focusing on this plan knowing other changes will present themselves, and with God's help I'll pick them off one by one. Chair five was far easier than I had ever envisioned.

"I'm a relatively focused person. I usually have a plan outlined for the next day as I prepare for bed each night. My problem was that the plan never included working on the diagnosis. It was organized but did not involve discipline to change the ministry. So chair number six is a matter of adjustment. I'm now disciplining my life around the plan. I always keep a tablet with me, so I can easily access important information, like my plan, my students' contact info, and my schedule of attending their events. I now spend fifteen minutes a day sending encouraging texts, Facebook messages, and tweets to students. I sometimes blanket them so regulars and visitors hear from me weekly and sometimes more. I daily—really, *daily*—review the videos and lecture notes from my public speaking track. And I've been bathing each one of my students in prayer each day so it's turned into delight and even habit. I was reminded by Hebrews 13:17 that I'll give an account to God for the students in this ministry. And I'm taking that convicting reminder seriously.

"Chair seven is also easier than I had envisioned. Already I'm nearly in a full-blown habit of declaring loving and powerful confessions over these students. From the first Psalm I love to say, 'My kids are oaks, planted by the rivers of water that bring forth fruit in their season and whatever they do prospers.'

"Every day, I like to say the following declarations:

#1 *God is granting me favor not only with these students I pastor but also with the youth community at large.*
#2 *God is filling chairs with students and filling students with himself.*
#3 *This is the Lord's ministry, and I am his under-shepherd. He receives the glory, and glory there will be.*

I have a few more also. I love what happens in my heart as I extend my faith.

"Some things can be measured but some really are subjective. Enthusiasm is a hard thing to measure. One simply knows when it's there and when it's not. One real determinant for me is body count. If I set out sixty-five chairs and twenty-nine people show up, I can easily measure the reality against my expectations. So, bodies and buy-in are what I find in chair number eight. Are the kids showing up, and are they owning and believing the vision? Another big measurement is the number of visitors brought by regulars. When students don't bring their friends, it's often because they don't believe in their student ministry, or worse, they are embarrassed. Chair number eight? Check.

"Excuses? How much time do you have? I don't know when I became a serial excuse-maker. Maybe as a small child. My parents told me when I was small and would hit my head on the coffee table, my loving grandmother would scold the table and give it a spanking. I'd feel better and sometimes spank it myself. Grammy thought she was being helpful. My dad wasn't crazy about this prospect. He thought it might make me crazy and called it 'Grammy's Going Postal Training Program'. It seems like I have been blaming people and stuff my whole life, including now: 'Grammy made me an excuse maker.'

"Here are some favorites:

'Ministry is a man's world. Of course it's harder for me. The kids don't respect my gender.'

'Being single is a tough hurdle to make.'

'No one trained me for these curve balls in ministry.'

Oh, that's just chapter one. Excuses are as natural and comfortable as my favorite jeans. One way I'm trying to destroy them is with pictures of great women of ministry I've placed near my makeup drawer. I call it my Inspiration Station. It was harder for most of them than it will ever be for me.

"I sit in chair number nine destroying these excuses one-by-one. When they rear their ugly heads like Jason in a horror movie, I just dunk them down again until they stop.

"Display? Well, whatever is on the other side of incredible is where this ministry is right now. That's the longitude and latitude of where this student minister is as well. The difference—the transformation—is profound. I cannot wait to share it."

ROLANDO

"I overheard a couple of people in the break room one day talking about a book called *The 5 Love Languages*. I bought a copy on the way home from work. I've been reading it on the down low. I don't want to announce to my wife or anybody else, 'Hey, I'm going to be a great husband.' I want to be it instead of promote it.

"I've learned from the book that my wife loves 'words of affirmation,' and I am not too good at giving them. I never really saw that stuff at home growing up, and I am a quiet processor. So now everyday I say or write to her something positive that I sincerely mean.

"I also 'check out' at home from the day's stress. I have purposed to 'check in' with my full concentration to what's going on at home. I heard an evangelist say something like, 'It's dumb for me to pray to be anointed only in the pulpit. I need to pray for the anointing more intensely when I put my hand on the front door knob.' That really resonated with me. So I've started doing that and talking more.

"I also spend more money on my marriage by taking my sweet wife somewhere every single week. Sometimes it's a big deal, and sometimes it's a small deal. I've gotten disciplined at it. I think, *If I can be good at work and disciplined there, I better be good where it really counts— home!*

"As I mentioned, I am not too verbal. Out-loud declarations seem awkward and odd to me, but I am making a few:

#1 *My marriage is a ten with God's help.*
#2 *I am Cheryl's (my wife) hero.*
#3 *We have a great marriage.*
#4 *Cheryl is truly happy.*

Even now it just feels weird. But I'm willing to feel weird to have a great marriage.

"The number one thing that will determine if this plan is working cannot be measured. It will be Cheryl's countenance. I want to lift her furrowed brow. If her face just lights up and blooms like a flower the way it used to, we will be winning. I also plan to pick a day on the calendar to take her out and ask her the same 'one-to-ten scale' question. That will be the other determinative. If she says ten, then I win. That is my new private motto and prayer: 'Lord, give me a ten to win.'

"Work, pressure, bills, responsibility, and blah blah blah excuses I am picking off like a sniper, one-by-one. Every lie should be met with the truth. I feel the prayer from my uncle as I get stronger, demolishing these excuses. I'm competitive by nature. I suppose most men are. So whenever an excuse rears its disgusting head, I remind myself that all great husbands have and overcome the same challenges.

"I hate liars, so I'm not going to tell a lie. This process has been hard. I've gotten discouraged at what I perceived as a profound lack of progress. But I possess a stubborn streak, and I just bowed my back and purposed to not give up. What has happened in our marriage must be a miracle."

11

DECISION
CHAIR THREE

"You do not want to leave too, do you?" Jesus asked the
Twelve. Simon Peter answered him, "Lord, to whom
shall we go? You have the words of eternal life."
(*John 6:67, 68*)

BRIDGE DAY

Every year on the third Saturday in October, Fayette County, West Virginia closes down its famed bridge over the New River for a special day. "Bridge Day" is the largest extreme sports event in the world. Hundreds of BASE jumpers and tens of thousands of spectators attend the event. The 876-foot-tall New River Gorge Bridge serves as the launch point for six hours of safe, legal BASE jumps (jumps from one of four categories: buildings, antennas, spans, and earth). This is the only day of the year traffic is shut down and spectators can safely and legally walk across the world's second-longest single-arch bridge.

I have attended the event twice. People stand on this perfectly secure structure, each with what looks like a rag, but is actually a parachute, in one hand. Of their own volition, they each step off. They step off into the abyss of 876 feet. EIGHT HUNDRED SEVENTY-SIX feet! They count, "One Mississippi, two Mississippi, three Mississippi, throw!" before opening their parachutes.

Most of them make it fine, and I suppose it must be a fun activity for them. Some jumpers break body parts like arms and legs. Some don't make it at all. Yes, people have died.

ESPN covers the event. The network puts a boom crane out from the bridge and lays down video of the daredevils. I could barely stand to look over the side when I attended. Merely observing nearly gave me dysentery, migraines, and other bad things.

Sometimes timid souls go to the edge and look back saying, "I don't think I'm going to do this. This is kind of scary."

Bystanders shout their encouragement. "You can do it!"

I'm shouting too. "Don't do it! Stay on the safe bridge. Live! Hey, life is good. Go buy a peach milkshake. It can change your life."

There is one thing that I've never seen happen at Bridge Day in West Virginia. No one has ever stepped off of the bridge, counted "One Mississippi," and then said, "No, I'm coming back up. I changed my mind," while turning and stepping back onto the bridge. Now, they might change their minds, even think that they would like to return, but they are not coming back up to bridge security. Once a BASE jumper steps off the edge of the bridge, that rag better hold him up because there is no turning back. The parachute is plans A through Z.

SIMON PETER JUMPED

In John chapter six, there was a parachute. The Lord gave a difficult word to his followers. Many people didn't like it, and they stopped walking with Jesus. John 6:66—an interesting reference number, don't you think?—says:

> *After this many of his disciples turned back and no longer walked with him. (ESV)*

Then Jesus pressed the remaining disciples. "You guys splitting, too?"

Peter had been standing in the jump line for quite a while. He had been taking inventory of his courage and his future. He had worked that question through in advance and revealed he had spent time in the most important chair of the entire process:

> *Simon Peter answered him, "Lord, to whom shall we go? You have the words of eternal life." (John 6:68 [ESV])*

Peter told Jesus that he had already jumped off the bridge.

MORE THAN PRAYER

Very few things on earth are more important than prayer. But this stop, this step, this chair probably is only a little more important. We have literally saved the best for last. Most of us know the changes we need to make in our lives. Diagnosis is not a problem. We dream about what it would be like to look better, feel better, have money, have fulfillment, and simply be better. Dreaming is not the problem. Chairs four through ten in this change process really do work in principle and function. However, they will *not* work without this most important chair of all. This is the chair of Decision.

OVER THE CLIFF

The old joke goes something like this: A man had fallen off of a cliff and was holding onto a root, suspended hundreds of yards above the earth. He prayed, "Lord, please help me. I don't want to die."

He heard a voice from Heaven saying, "I am here, my son. Trust me. Let go. I will save you."

After a few seconds of consideration, the man yelled, "Is there anyone else up there?"

Heroin users can pray, and God will hear their prayers. But God chooses mostly, with few exceptions, to answer the prayers of those who have made *decisions*.

DECISIONS > GOALS

A decision is far greater than a goal. Goals are like those resolutions we make at the beginning of the year. "This year, I will run a marathon (I've never even run around the block), learn Latin (until the third day when I find out it is a dead language), and build a house for Habitat for Humanity (though I have never touched a hammer and I hate to sweat)." By January 9, we are back to Cheetos and *Law and Order* marathons.

We make goals to lose weight, save money, read books, pray prayers, and so on. And those goals are often not worth the paper they are written on. They're more like hopes, wishes, or mystical, invisible lottery tickets. "I'll write this down and hope I win. If I don't, oh well, I'll play next year."

A decision, however, ultimately births this declaration: "I've trained, prepared, double-checked, prayed, updated my will, focused, prayed some more, and now I hope this parachute works! Wheeeee!"

That's the place we need to arrive if we expect profound transformation in our lives. A demeanor that with every moment declares, "I'm not leaving this place until I'm different."

HILLBILLY WISDOM

I have a deep and profound respect for people in Appalachia. They are a deep-feeling and sincere folk. I've met more than one that takes some pride in the moniker "hillbilly." A great leader I met there, Marvin Dennis, told me something years ago I've not forgotten. He probably heard it somewhere (maybe the old Alcoholics Anonymous saying or from Henry Cloud) but I first heard it from his lips: "Joe, no major change will ever take place *until the pain of remaining the same is greater than the pain of the change.*"

Let's revisit that before we read another thing. "A major change will never be made until the pain of remaining the same is greater than the pain of the change." I have found that statement to be true in all areas:

"I'll stay fat until being fat is so uncomfortable that it's more painful than the work of losing weight."

"We'll be late every day for work until a supervisor makes it painful, uncomfortable, and unpleasant."

People stay on drugs until the poverty, broken relationships, prison, sickness, and heartache are more horrible than the detox.

This is called *decision*.

ROCK IN SHOE

Have you ever been walking when you realize a rock is in your shoe? Sometimes people will walk a little while with rock accompaniment because it's not that uncomfortable at first. But with the increased steps or the shifting position of the pebble, the walker often crosses a threshold of discomfort. That person will finally stop and get the shoe off immediately. If a bystander sees this transaction at that exact moment, it may be mistaken for some kind of spastic seizure. If a person is late paying bills every single month, the late bill program will continue until a threshold is passed. Late fees, interest, reputation, legal notices, and such make the pain of remaining the same greater than the pain of the change. My great friend Lee McBride calls those fees "idiot tax." When someone pays enough idiot tax, he warms to the idea of transformation.

ORGANIZATIONS, TOO

If a person is running a florist shop that needs improvement, that "pain of the change" saying applies. The business may just rock along like it has for the previous twenty years. When the status quo becomes too uncomfortable, the third chair of decision will be a beginning point of better business. That's a difficult place to stop, especially if things are "not too bad." I've also heard it said, "If you keep doing the things you have always done, you will keep getting the things you have always gotten."

Different things happen after decisions are made. Churches that just repeat last year's calendar and hope for a dozen more at the Harvest Festival usually get about that and not much else. Hungry churches that decide and demand change produce effective results.

Leadership knows what it wants, and leadership is sure it wants it. Change requires work. It requires real work, and that's the reason more people don't linger in this chair. The mere prospect of the ramifications of change is simply daunting.

Youth groups, civic organizations, little leagues, and any other organizations need to make *corporate decisions* if they expect corporate change. Branding, values, mission, culture. All of it's affected by decision. President Bush called himself "the decider." Too many times there isn't a decider but a collector. A collector of information, of opinion polls and general consensus. I'm not sure where I heard this, but I like it: "In any park in any city there stands no statue of a committee." Some *person* has to decide. The person then needs to sell others on the decision.

SOME THINGS ARE WORTH IT

A few decades ago, a friend of mine, Robby, had to leave a pretty great job working with teenagers affording him lots of golf time and freedom. He was then forced to go back into the classroom after years away from it. Things had changed. Culture was different. Students were different. And Robby was shocked. Two days into the career change one of these new generation students cussed him out using some "big boy" cuss words. Robby, rather short in stature compared to the large student, seriously invaded the young man's space near a locker. He looked up at the offender and said, "Son, some things are worth going to jail for." The student immediately took on a whole new demeanor.

Here is a very intriguing Bible verse that's one of my personal favorites:

> **And they have overcome (conquered) him by means of the blood of the Lamb and by the utterance of their testimony, _for they did not love and cling to life even when faced with death_ [holding their lives cheap till they had to die for their witnessing].** (Revelation 12:11 [Amp.])

Are some things worth going to jail for? Probably. Are some things worth going to Hell for? Never. Are some things worth dying for? Surely. When we are willing to die to our own goals and carnal desires in order to go "from glory to glory," real change is conceived.

"I don't care what it costs me, I'm going to change. If it costs everything, this change must be made." That attitude is the onramp of everything beginning to finish differently.

NO ELECTRICITY

In April 2007, I decided to jump off the bridge. I decided to travel and speak around the country full time and literally by faith. In some church denominations this career choice is called "evangelist." Others have called it "exhorter." Some might call it "crazy." The economy had tanked. Not many people dared to pursue this career in our denomination, the Assemblies of God, as I mentioned in chapter seven.

When I jumped, my eyes were wide open. I had first-hand knowledge of the lack of glamour this path holds. There are very few luxury hotels and fewer big payouts. I've experienced my share of dumps: "Your check is in the mail," and the dreaded, "We wish it could be more." When I hear that last one, my silent response is, "Not as much as I do and not as much as the electric company does."

I experienced some dark days and weeks as an evangelist. It was dark. Spiritually, emotionally, and sometimes literally. My family had to spend at least a couple of nights in the dark at times until I could get the lights back on. Meanwhile I waited on that "check in the mail" or tried to find any group that would let me tell jokes for a tip. I hate financial setbacks, so I was doing a lot of hating during this period of my life. Evangelists may receive a wonderful offering one Sunday and then barely anything for weeks on end.

On April 20, at about five am (the date is easy to remember because it's my wife's birthday), I was on my way to a prayer room in our town when I heard from God. I heard in my spirit: "Haggai two." I heard just the reference. I was excited because I was desperate, and the Lord had spoken to me. I couldn't remember what Haggai 2 said, but I knew it was going to say something to me that day. I couldn't wait to get into that room and open my Bible. Imagine my chagrin when I read a chapter that basically says, "You don't have enough." That was obvious!

In this passage God is chastising the people. Their twenty units of measure were worth only ten. Their work was smitten with "blasting winds." They were literally fruitless. I looked at the first chapter later, and it described my plight:

> **He who earns, earns wages to put into a purse with holes.** (Haggai 1:6b [New American Standard Bible])

I literally prayed, "I'm an idiot. I deserve a spanking. Go ahead, Lord."

I felt like I was living what I've heard Dr. Mark Rutland pray: "Better a word of rebuke from you than rivers of praise from the lips of men."

Then verse 2:19b hit me:

> **Yet from this day forward I will bless you.** (NASB)

That verse blew up inside my heart and mind. I literally started pumping my fist like I had won a game with a last-second shot. The verse changed me because I believed it. I started living like it was a done deal. When I worked out, I quoted one word from that verse with each rep of the weights I was lifting. It became part of me.

On April 20, 2009, every single account I had added together (including children's accounts) was less than 190 dollars. Our financial situation has never been so bleak, as in not one single day since that time right up to this moment. We are not rich televangelists with private jets and entourages, by any stretch. However, today we enjoy some miraculous margin in this ministry as we try to win thousands of people for God.

MISSIONARIES & MARGIN

This margin happened because of decision. Two years later, at the end of 2011, I jumped off another bridge. I sat in the third chair once again. I had been around this chair of decision for quite a while. I knew a financial transformation had to happen for us to survive and thrive. My thirtieth anniversary as a Christian would be in 2012. So Cecilia and I decided that, no matter what, we would give more to the Kingdom of God in that calendar year than we had ever given before. I am embarrassed to admit that the following philosophical change took so long to happen.

We have always tithed—given 10 percent of our gross income to the Lord. (I've never met a person who loved to tithe more than my wife Cecilia. It's *truly* an act of worship with her.) A thought hit me, and I'm sure it was born out of the promise from God in April 2009: *I want our home to be blessed. Why not tithe on the ministry before I pay my salary?*

So we began giving to missionaries from our ministry funds before we paid our salary. Then we still paid our tithe. We began to support missionaries in Israel, India, Egypt, Tallahassee, North Carolina church planting, Bogota, Columbia, and Europe. As we made those monthly commitments, something supernatural happened: financial margin. No more living honorarium to honorarium. We had had to decide to give even when it seemed it could be the end of us. Instead, it was the beginning of something beautiful. I've heard my friend Gary Sapp say, "If God can get it through you, he will surely get it to you."

I recently had this thought about giving: *Great givers are great receivers. Correctly motivated givers are the best receivers in order that they might become the greatest givers.*

This third-chair experience transformed forever our lives and ministry.

OTHER THIRD CHAIRS
Small decisions over time create great differences. Here are a few others I've made along the way:

"I won't touch the remote control of televisions in hotels when I travel." (If my family travels with me they can control the television—especially for ball games!) There is so much ridiculous programming that even the most innocently motivated find it distracting. I got so sick of the junk I decided to eliminate it completely. Result? Greater anointing and concentration.

"I will fast every Sunday when I'm preaching." I picked this up from a pastor friend, James Longmate in Arkansas. Result? More faith and power when I preach.

"I will not go a single night without praying with my wife." I decided this after I preached the funeral of my hero Jimmy Griggs. I'd been a little hit or miss with the evening prayers, especially if I had had a busy travel schedule. I decided I'd begin this prayer the way Jimmy used to pray for his daughter. "Dear Lord God..." Normally I pray to the Father or sometimes to Jesus. I wanted to keep this tradition from a great intercessor alive. Result? A sweet intimacy with the Lord and an awareness of our heritage.

PAIN MOTIVATION

In the American healthcare system, we patients graduate from a big room with random other ailing folks to individual little rooms, alone. "The doctor will be with you shortly." Charts. Alarming posters. Various medical paraphernalia. Sometimes there is a scale on the wall. On this scale, numbers are listed one through ten. Sometimes it's a progression of smiling faces to frowning faces. We are to use it to assess our pain level:

"Doctor, I am feeling, uh, about a, say, 6ish to 7ish."

"Doc, I am between a three-quarter frown and a sixty-six percent frown."

You and I will not change until the pain of remaining the same is greater than the transformation discomfort. Where are you on the pain chart? If it's a three, chances are you'll say, "Pass the Cheetos," and keep on rolling down Status Quo Street. Are you uncomfortable enough in your present "degree of glory" to go to another glory? If you are experiencing that level of discomfort in your present situation, make a decision.

Simon Peter jumped because he didn't want to fish for fish anymore. Fishing for men was more appealing. When Jesus decided to go raise Lazarus from the dead, his disciple Thomas said (in doubt but in chair number three, nonetheless):

Let us also go, that we may die with him. *(John 11:16b)*

Now we're getting somewhere. We don't walk around with a death wish. We change when we have a life wish that expresses itself in whatever position it takes.

Make a choice. Have a purpose. What needs to change? As long as we live, we make changes. Make good ones. The scale, the garage, the home atmosphere, the team, the habit, the devotional life, the ministry, the sales figures, the academics, everything can experience the possibility of transformation. The true starting point is in that uncomfortable chair, Decision. Sit in it quickly, stand up out of it, and jump into the next degree of glory.

12

BE TRANSFORMED
GLORY TO GLORY

For the trumpet will sound, the dead will be raised
imperishable, and we will be changed.
(*1 Corinthians 15:52b*)

IT WORKS

I've come to the end of this book to bring about full disclosure. You don't really need to literally sit down in ten different chairs to improve your life. I suppose alcoholics do not literally take twelve steps. Bill Gates, Warren Buffet, Lebron James, and Taylor Swift will never write autobiographies citing how that third chair stop was their catalyst.

However, the principles of this book are universal. An old university professor of mine often said, "All truth is God's truth." Truth works. Truth works for the atheist, the evangelical, the confused, and the monks. A plan is a powerful thing. This plan will work for you. Modify it, and adapt it to your situation. Pull from these pages motivation to get to another place in life. Find from the examples below an inspiration to display the change you want.

ROLANDO

"If I hadn't seen it with my own eyes I'm not sure I would've believed it. My dear wife Cheryl has bloomed like a flower. She doesn't sit in front of the computer every night until she is too exhausted to stand it another second. She did that before because she knew she was getting nothing out of me other than nods and grunts in response to her attempts at conversation. It's like we're dating again. She drops notes in my pockets. I blush and giggle when I read them. We can't wait to tell each other about our days. I listen because I'm genuinely interested. We are no longer business associates at Our House, Incorporated, but we are submitted partners, parents, loving spouses, and sweet companions. I'm interested in what she's interested in, what I previously considered some of the most boring things in the world. Cheryl has offered to do some of my 'out in the woods man stuff.' (Cheryl in camouflage and hunting? I'm still mulling that one over!)

"Here is the proof of the pudding, as they say. I surprised her a little while back. I picked her up from work and brought an overnight bag. We went to a local hotel where I had already put a dozen roses on the dresser and a new dress for her on the bed. She went in the restroom and tried it on right away. She screamed a little scream. I was scared because I thought she must hate it. When she opened the door there were tears in her eyes.

'Why did you scream?' I asked her.

'Because it fits perfectly!' she cried. 'How did you...?'

"To be honest it didn't cost very much, and the reason it fit was because her sister told me exactly what size went with what brands she told me to look for.

"I had also placed tickets to the theater on her pillow. We hurried to get ready for the curtain. I am a little embarrassed to say she loves the theater, but that was my first show ever. We made the show in plenty of time.

"Afterward we enjoyed a dinner of her favorite food, crab legs. I was trying to summon the courage during dinner to ask her what our marriage was on a scale of one to ten. It wasn't really a fair time to ask the question because I'd stacked the deck. While I was waiting for an opening in the conversation, she looked into my eyes and said one word: 'Ten.'

'Excuse me?' I asked.

'Ten,' she repeated.

'What are you talking about?' (Was she reading my mind?)

'Rolando, our marriage is a ten, and it's not because of the dress or the theater. It has been a ten for quite a while now. I've just been looking for a special time to tell you, and I think I found one.' Score! Changed. Now there were tears in my eyes.

"I'm enjoying the fruit of a moment of decision made early one Saturday morning over a year ago as I sat in the woods hunting deer.

I had assessed that Cheryl and I were two married single people doing our own things. That's what our marriage had become. We were at the same dance but moving awkwardly to two different songs. It hit me that we were out of sync, and if I let it remain we would soon be out of time to save our marriage. In a tree stand waiting for passing deer that morning, I made a decision. It was a firm decision. It was almost as strong as any big life decision I've ever made. If we were going to dance to two different tunes, it would only happen after I expended every single ounce of energy I would pour out every single day for the rest of my life. The tears at a fancy dinner table really were the result of other tears—of regret and frustration—shed in a deer stand early one Saturday morning a year before."

JANE

"Welcome to my dream. The nightmare came first. That was the nightmare of adjusting the literal chairs in my meeting room. I used to have this absurd philosophy of youth ministry. I would put out the chairs for the number of students I had 'faith' for. Sixty-five kids! Put them up. 'If you build it they will come.' Not so much. They didn't come. When twenty kids showed up in a room of sixty-five chairs, it looked like a funeral service for the town weirdo. They looked like hostages waiting for the government to send the troops in for a rescue. I could see the question in their eyes: 'Why does Mom make me come here?'

"I began to be practical without losing my faith. The plan I received in chair five worked just like I declared it would in chair six. I began to strategically put out about seven chairs fewer than I extended my faith for. I liked the panic of momentary 'standing room only' atmosphere. Imagine the enthusiasm and energy in a room when not sixty-five students but ninety-one students showed up. I always keep stacks of chairs close and in the corner. The expressions on the faces of my student leaders were priceless as they scrambled to get those extra chairs in place to accommodate the crowd. Easily accessible 'spare chairs' gave a 'look what God is doing' sensation to everyone.

"Now I'm in the seat of demonstration. God is on display. There is order, there is love, and there is spiritual hunger and a deep sense of community. The journey really was every bit as great as the destination. But make no mistake, this destination is absolutely wonderful. I stay overwhelmed.

"Chair number three was the catalyst, of course. I got close to this chair several times. I got close to it during staff meetings when the regular reports were given. It seemed everyone was experiencing growth, revival, world-class ministry, and then there was me, 'Sister Status Quo.' (I'm honest to a fault. I wasn't going to spin averages. Averages can only be spun so long until smart people sniff out the truth.) I got close to the third chair in my prayer times when I sensed the Spirit calling me to something greater.

"My great epiphany about my need came on a Friday night. I was going through the motions, and as I walked through the parking lot of our high school football game, I saw something out of my peripheral vision. It was something in the back of an extended cab truck. I turned to see a couple of guys who had attended our student ministry in the past—not regulars but regular visitors—were in there tipping up a bottle and laughing. On the campus of *my* school, two of *my* kids were kicking back what looked to be whiskey. It was a holy indignation that came upon me. It was a brokenness and a—for lack of better term—repentance.

"I couldn't even pay for my ticket at the gate. I stood in the grass by a chain link fence, staring at the visiting stands, and wept at my inability to reach those young men with the powerful life-changing message of a resurrected Savior. Something happened to me in that moment. Beyond emotion, beyond sorrow, and beyond the anger that did eventually visit me, a giant switch was activated in my heart. I said out loud, 'No more!' I said it so loud and so many times that I hoped nobody could see or hear me. No more! No more going through the motions. No more apathy. No more playing church politics, church games, and churchy culture. Real power now. Real presence now. Real life now. I demanded it of myself and of my atmosphere. In the future, there would inevitably be fringe kids—and possibly core kids—drinking whiskey. But they would have to do so by going around a vibrant, dynamic, and Spirit-charged student ministry.

"I believe when I left that chain link fence at the thirty-yard line that night, the Lord began to give me the places where my feet touched, just like the Bible says. And as they say, the rest is history; well, it's a history we're writing each week. We're going to future degrees of glory."

WHAD'A YA HAVE?
The Varsity, a restaurant in Atlanta, is a great landmark. It's truly an iconic southern establishment. Millionaires and homeless people

eat there. Politicians and pimps. Presidents have visited. When you walk in, there looks to be a row of cash registers as long as a football field. There are employees behind each, and they all yell the same phrase to everyone: "Whad'a ya have?!"

And, buddy, you better know what you want. If you pose a, "What's good here?" question, you may get barked at.

I've heard them order a Yankee to the back of the line to figure it out. "Next!! Whad'a ya have?"

The examples in this book are sort of modern parables of people in various stages of life. Young and older. Male and female. But the Word of God is living, active, and historically factual. The Word of Nehemiah is one very cool example of the change process. We have established that he had diagnosed disaster. The third chair came about in a moment. And sometimes that's how it happens. In a single moment.

Here is Nehemiah's moment. He had been sad in the king's presence. He probably knew pouting was a bad idea around royalty, and I doubt he was some drama queen. The diagnosis was just heartbreaking to him, and he couldn't hide it. Nehemiah 2:4a says:

The king said to me, "What is it you want?"

Right here is the difference between dreaming in perpetuity and real success. There was a real risk in Nehemiah's telling the king he needed time away. The king didn't have a royal policy manual with paid leave and vacation days, and he could have interpreted a request to leave as an insult.

Nehemiah's bridge moment was when he uttered these words:

> ***If it pleases the king and if your servant has found favor in his sight, let him send me to the city...so that I can rebuild it.*** (*Nehemiah 2:5*)

What a courageous decision. His sad countenance reveals that the pain of remaining the same was greater than the pain of the change. Immediately that moving sidewalk took effect. A plan involving time away, letters to governors, timber, and all sorts of strategy presented itself.

We know Nehemiah was a man of prayer. I imagine he was also a man of faith-filled declaration and inspiring leadership. He rejected out-of-hand any and all excuses that were present. And many were present:

The devastation was too massive.

There weren't enough helpers.

There wasn't enough money.

He already had a good job.

It was dangerous, really dangerous.

This was Nehemiah's excuse busting attitude:

> ***But I said, "Should a man like me run away?"***
> *(Nehemiah 6:11)*

Verse twenty-five says he completed the wall. He realized the Dream. He changed the diagnosis to a display of the power of God. Every surrounding nation became afraid and lost its self-confidence. They all realized God had helped the change take place.

Nehemiah's looking at a rebuilt wall was the absolute direct result of making a decision in the king's presence and going for it. In the New Testament Jesus often asked, "What do you want me to do for you?" If the Lord asks you what you want, are you prepared to answer?

SANDY
"Chair number nine is my enemy. It's my impossibility. Have you ever played that arcade game where the animals pop up, and you have to smack them with a mallet? They are all over the machine, and you can't get them fast enough. That's how it is with me and excuses. I smack one and another pops up.

'Your dad was gone all the time.' Whack!

'That boy broke your heart.' Whack!

'Why did my cousin give me that first joint?' Smack!

'It's in my system, and it is who I am. I can't change it now. Too far gone.' Whack! Smack! Whack.

"I am done trying to smack them; there are too many. So I imagined myself putting some C-4 explosive on the excuse machine to just blow it—my language is changing—to smithereens.

"Twelve months without a joint, a needle, a bottle, a cigarette even. I confess I drink a little coffee and soda without guilt. But I feel great. I mean in the literal dictionary definition: *great*. I am breathing deeply. I ran a mile. It hurt the most beautiful hurt I have ever felt deep down in my lungs. I have money—not much, but I have it for the first time. Weird. I have dignity. Wonderfully weird.

"A boy from back in high school became a Christ-follower (I used to call it a 'religious freak'), and we've been talking. He is the real article. A man who loves God. Who knows? I just know that a year and a half ago, a conversation with such an amazing person would have been impossible. I'm changed. Announce it, display it, shout it from the roof. I'm transformed. God does miracles, and I see one in the mirror every time I brush my teeth.

"Chair number three? Chair number three. Whew. That was a 'come-to-Jesus' chair, as my new friend says a lot. It nearly killed me. I had worn out Diagnosis and Dream. I sat in those so long I nearly broke them down. I saw this chair—Decision—from a distance. I had no idea I could sit in it because I didn't even know how I could get to it. I wanted this chair so badly. GPS, Mapquest, and Rand McNally could not get me to it, I was convinced. But I was motivated by an invisible hand to find it. I was motivated by the pain. Truly the pain of remaining the same was greater than the pain of the change.

"One night—one absolutely gloriously horrifying night—I found a place of decision. I didn't care anymore about the cost of change. I didn't care to the point of death. In a friend's apartment. In her daughter's bedroom. I had been given a 'one night pass.' That's how she said it. And I heard her lock her own bedroom door, her daughter in there with her, when she went to bed. I sat on the floor too numb to weep any more tears. 'My God, my friends are terrified of me. They don't want their children around me.' And I was terrified of myself. 'What have I become?' was not cliché with me. It was my profile picture. One of my wacked out religious friends had given me a piece of paper, and I saw it that night sticking out of my ratty purse. On the paper were these words that I later discovered to be a Bible verse from Revelation 12:11:

They triumphed over him
  by the blood of the Lamb
  and by the word of their testimony;

they did not love their lives so much
  as to shrink from death.

I was so creeped out by it when she gave it to me that I was angry. I really thought I had tossed it. But in that room, that night, with that verse, I found the chair. I climbed right up in it and made the best call of my life: 'I will change if it kills me. I am not shrinking from death.' I knew if I didn't stop and make this decision my lifestyle would really kill me. I found the road to all things good right there. My running shoes, my savings account, and my new friend all were born the night I decided to change no matter the cost."

GIDEON

God told Gideon to tear down a false idol to Baal (Judges 6) and to tear down the wicked and profane Asherah pole. He had to demolish excuses before demolishing idolatry:

"That's my daddy's pole, my bubba's pole, all my cousins' pole, and all my buddies' pole. They are gonna be ticked!"

He tore down the excuse. Then, afraid of his family and the town, at night, he tore down the pole. When he took ten employees on that trip, he was launching out of that third chair of decision.

In chapter seven, he rescued his people miraculously from the enemy. That was the display. The victory really came at a midnight decision.

KEVIN

"I spend a pretty good amount of time in chair number nine. I have always made excuses. I thought they were pretty good ones. I know now they stink. So I wrote them down:

#1 I never had a big brother to play with me.
#2 Dad could never afford to send me to football camps.
#3 No one has ever pushed me.

#4 The coaches never invited me to try out like I saw them doing to the bigger kids.
#5 I have bad DNA.

"I took these five, and five other ones, out to the backyard one night. I built a little fire in our fire pit. I repeated each one, called it "liar," and then burned it. I felt so good doing it.

"I love chair number ten. I especially love it on game day. I am leaner than I have ever been. I am faster. Not only am I on the Northside football team, but my coach told me I'll contribute. Even if I don't start, I'll be a part of the outcome of each game. 'It's not who starts the game, it's who finishes it,' he said. He likes my attitude and my work ethic. I have to say, I like this change, too. I'm glad I tried because I would've always hated not trying and wondering about what might have been.

"Chair number three was the biggest deal. I know it was. I sat in this chair in a weird location. Actually, it wasn't a chair. It was a tree stump. Mom and I had had a stupid fight about how much video gaming I was doing. I slammed the door (which I got in trouble for later) and walked out into some woods by the house. I sat down and thought about the fight and thought about what good all that gaming was doing. I was good at a couple of games, but who really cared? Big deal. When I thought, *Big deal*, I wondered if anything was a big deal. As I sat right there on that stump, like a bolt of lightning this thought hit me: *Being on the football team would be a big deal.* When I got my rump off that stump I had made up my mind to do whatever it took to have a chance to play football.

"Nobody is as excited about me making the team as my Nana. She might be more excited than I am. She told her Kevin Prayer Team about it, and one of the members—or whatever they are called—said something pretty cool. He said, 'There never would have been a football jersey without a made-up-mind stump.' I think he's right. That stump plus all their prayers.

PRODIGAL

The story of the Prodigal Son is both a parable and the Word. He represents so many of us. His wasted life was a low-tide, high-tide rhythm of diagnosis and dream. The end of that great story is a fatted calf, a ring, and a party. The food did not happen until this happened:

> ***When he came to his senses, he said, "...I will set out and go back to my father and say to him: 'Father, I have sinned against heaven and against you...'" So he <u>got up and went</u> to his father.*** *(Luke 15:17, 18, 20)*

That one decision to *get up* is the reason he would taste veal, enjoy a ring, finally get some shoes, and see people who loved him (with the possible exception of a jealous brother).

This process works. Gideon is a witness. Nehemiah is a record of its success. The Prodigal Son is a testimony.

CONCLUSION

CHANGE NOW

Beloved, now are we the sons of God, and it doth not yet
appear what we shall be...
(1 John 3:2 [KJV])

TOSSING LIQUOR

As I was in the process of finishing this book, two interesting things happened on the same night. First, I went outside to take a call from a former student of mine, now an adult. He was sick of his drug and alcohol addiction. He wanted some suggestions about where to go to get clean and sober. I've helped place many students over the years in the program our character Sandy referenced in her testimony. Teen Challenge is pretty successful for getting men, women, boys, and girls out from under life controlling addictions. I was so proud this young man was honest and hungry for a change. I thought, *It was the third chair that brought about this conversation.* Same was uglier than change for this young man on this dark night.

The second thing happened when I came back into the house. A scene played on a movie my wife and I were watching. It was so eerily similar to the conversation I had just had, it couldn't have been co-incidental. A man eaten up with alcoholism was going through every cabinet and hiding place in his house looking for liquor. He poured every can and bottle's contents down the drain and filled a trashcan with the empty containers. For the second time in one night it hit me: *The third chair brought this character to this action.*

SAME has to get uglier than CHANGE for all of us. Once that switch goes off a civil servant can build a wall, the dumbest dummy can save a nation, a kid can make a team, an alcoholic can become a teetotaler, a minister can fill a room, a lost son can come home, and YOU can transform.

"SHAKEY" GENERATIONS

Jimmy Griggs, my father-in-law, was nicknamed Shakey. It was an apt moniker. He shook the change in his pocket quite frequently and generally had a full-body twitch of one sort or another. At his funeral, a speaker joked that Jimmy wore out his clothes from the inside. Shakey's world was shaken on that fateful day Anne had the surgery. *Same* switched with *change* that day. He knew he had to switch gears and switch directions.

When James Albert "Shakey" Griggs sat in the third chair of decision in 1969, he didn't know the world would be profoundly better because of it. But God knew. God knew decades before that Jimmy Griggs would have seven grandchildren who would all know and serve the Lord. One grandson is a pastor. Another goes on missions trips and is a great athlete. Two are budding artists for God's glory. The baby has won poetry awards. One granddaughter is an award-winning speaker and, as I write this conclusion, got on an airplane for Nicaragua to speak about the Lord and to minister hope. Our decisions reverberate through generations.

BORN TWICE

I was eighteen. I was angry. Angry at the divorce of my adopted parents. Angry about being given away. Angry at abuse as a small child. Angry about being poor. Angry and missing my adopted mom. I was confused. I was raised with a heightened sense of sensuality. Conversations and concepts about sexuality from older men in the extended family got confusing. I was raised witnessing rage. Dysfunction was my companion.

I so honor my adopted parents now. They rescued me at the age of three. My adopted mom gave me the work ethic and the sense of integrity I have to this day. My adopted dad made some poor decisions I know he probably regretted later in life. Or at least he regretted the way he made them. I have regrets, too. I don't throw stones. I bless his memory. He died far too early at the age of sixty-three.

We moved a lot. It built character and crumbled some relationships. I went to four high schools in four years in four states: Missouri, Florida, Alabama, and Georgia. Angry and confused, I went to Mr. Luther Reeder's math class at seven thirty am one day in November 1980. I will share what happened that day in later projects, but the bottom line is Mr. Luther Reeder took an interest in my life that day. He invited me to work at his Opelika, Alabama, farm on Saturdays and go to church on Sundays. In the summer of 1982, because of this invitation, my life was transformed.

It was during that summer I learned of a Savior. I learned that God had a son named Jesus. Jesus had always been forever like God has always been. I learned that He volunteered to leave the great glory of Heaven and come to Earth on and for purpose. I learned that Jesus lived a perfect life. He never had a sinful thought. I had millions, it seemed. He never did a sinful thing. I was always and always doing sinful things. Jesus never said a sinful word. I constantly did. The amazing thing to me is that Jesus volunteered to become that nasty sin for me. Like a tsunami washing over me was this prospect:

> **God made him who had no sin to be sin for us, so that in him we might become the righteousness of God.** (*2 Corinthians 5:21*)

I could hardly get my mind around Jesus becoming anger, malice, wrath, discord, perversion, enmity, strife, prejudice, unbelief, disloyalty, hatred, adultery, witchcraft, deceit, and every other filthy thing. All I had to do was believe it and accept his sacrifice as a free gift. It was the greatest deal I had ever heard about.

I prayed a prayer something like the one below. If you have never prayed this prayer or one like it, I invite you to do so now by faith:

Lord Jesus, thank you for dying on that horrible cross and volunteering for a horrible beating. I know you did it because you loved me. And I know you could have stopped it at any time. I believe you died for me. I receive you as my Savior. I accept you. Please live inside of my life. I confess you with my mouth and believe in you in my heart. Thank you for going to purchase a place in Heaven for me that you offer as a free gift. Help me to live for you all the days of my life.

Amen.

So I did it. I accepted the deal. When I did, the greatest change in the world happened to me. It was a promised change. It was a powerful change. I transformed like Jimmy Griggs and like the Prodigal Son. My hate changed to love. My confusion turned to destiny. My pain turned into purpose.

Whatever change you need to make, decide to do it. Go through the cabinets and hiding places with deliberate intensity and fill up a bag with your valueless trash. Pursue the prize. Ask God to help you. His Spirit is mighty and wonderful. I leave you with a promise and a provocative prospect from the Bible. Here is your promise:

> *Therefore, if anyone is in Christ, he is a new creation. The <u>old has passed away</u>; behold, <u>the new has come</u>.* (2 Corinthians 5:17 [ESV])

And here is your provocative prospect:

> *The Spirit of the Lord will come powerfully upon you, and you will prophesy with them; <u>and you will be changed into a different person</u>.* (1 Samuel 10:6)

Be new.

Be changed.

Be transformed.

To contact Joe Phillips, you can reach him in the following ways:

Website: www.joephillipsministries.com

Address: PO Box 6193, Concord, NC 28027

Facebook: Joe Phillips Ministries

Twitter: @Revrollinjoe

Email: joe@joephillipsministries.com

35765422R00097

Made in the USA
Middletown, DE
14 October 2016